CUSTARD
'N'
SERVICE

AMANDA AUBREY-BURDEN

ISBN:9781549860423
ISBN-13: 9781549860423

DEDICATION

The 10ft Amazonian Woman.

CONTENTS

ACKNOWLEDGMENTS

All the friends, bosses and customers who made life working in
CUSTARD N SERVICE a pleasure.
Thank you!

i

THE NANNY FACTOR

When I left school I never thought for one moment that I
would become a 10ft Amazonian Woman. When asked what
careers I was interested in pursuing, my two prime choices
were either to join the army, or become a long-distance lorry
driver.

Now if you think about it, the choices are as interesting as
they are far-flung. The former is about discipline, training,
and working as part of a team. The latter; a more
independent role that would also entail training and
discipline – but that is where the comparisons end and I
ended up in neither! My dreams of adventures in the military
field, or else on the dusty roads overseas were diminished as
I embarked upon a modern life of service instead!

Whether it was looking after peoples' children, caring for
dear old ladies, or simply working the pumps in a bar, I
embarked upon a medley of roles that saw me peel potatoes
for five hundred in a dank, back room, to dressing a lady for
the day ahead complete with twinset and pearls and a dash of
red lippy.

As I ebbed and flowed below stairs and above them in
various establishments, it soon became clear that one
required a multitude of talents. It also soon became apparent

that a life in service was an adventure all of its own, and that you didn't need to be in the army to be shouted at or find drama on the road when you were at the mercy of the beast we call 'Customer Service.'

And so it began, at the tender age of fourteen when I was entrusted with the care of two little poppet's who were a pleasure rather than a chore. My foray into childcare became a regular stint that lasted for the next three years when my loyalty could be held by an over-flowing sweetie tin and a fried egg sandwich.

It was also around this time I was taught how to play chess by the eldest of my charges. She was six and extremely savvy, and bossed me into teaching her a few dance routines in exchange for the intricacies of check-mate. Having never ventured beyond the dubious delights of draughts and monopoly, how could I resist!

So as time went on, word got around that for a couple of quid and a full belly I was amenable and available and could give Mary Poppins a run for her money. I may not have had a magic brolly or the dulcet tones of the lovely Julie Andrews, but I had imagination and lots of it. And there are few things more appealing to the little people than an adult who makes being an adult look fun!

Therein began the first of many jobs that saw me grow from a juvenile version of Nanny McPhee into a versatile and (occasionally) competent contributor to a life in modern service!

As it began with the children it's only fair I start with them. Yet my role as an unqualified child-minder with no actual idea of childcare was as interesting as it was enlightening. Back in those days (I make it sound like a century, but it was nearly half a one - eek!) there were no such things as DRB checks and references. If the family liked your face and you looked trustworthy enough – the job was yours. Then off the parents would trot for a night out, happy in the knowledge that their children, house, and all their worldly possessions in the fledgling hands of a competent teenager.

Looking back on it, the trust was absolutely phenomenal - and to be fair I took my duties seriously and would continue to do so as long as the sweetie-tin was kept replenished.

Also these baby-sitting gigs could pay very well and there were always people looking out for a mini Mary Poppins. It was a path I believed I could embark upon as dreams of being yelled at on a parade ground or trundling miles upon the open road disappeared like a morning mist.

So I decided to take things one step further by spending my week of school work experience with the infants of my old primary school and I loved it!

But then what wasn't there to enjoy? Some of my happiest childhood memories were in this place.

Making collages and playing games, singing, reading, story-telling and charging around the playground – it was like a second childhood to me and I embraced every aspect with great enthusiasm. Being still quite young myself I blithely ignored the signs as the teachers muttered and shook their heads. Doubtless they were counting down the days, but the children were enthralled by my high spirits; I was like a renegade Pied Piper and I *still* didn't get the hint when it was suggested to me that perhaps I should re-consider a career in the army.

The week flew by but I thoroughly enjoyed it – I also took the opportunity to settle an old score with one of the teachers who didn't remember me but I remembered *her*. Children don't forget how an adult can make them feel – especially when they're just five years old in their first week of school.

This particular teacher was one of the stricter ones, prim,

slap-happy, and thankfully was never mine. She acquainted herself with me, however, when I dared to venture into 'her' cloakroom. My lovely teacher seeing me liberally covered in paint (I loved art!) had sent me down to the cloakroom to wash my hands, but there was no soap so I did what I thought was the next best thing.

I went off in search of the next one down the hall and hey-presto, a tiny tablet on every sink so I got stuck in.

I had just managed to work up a good lather when Miss Slap-Happy came in like an avenging angel. Her fury was on a par with Vesuvius – you'd have thought I'd piddled on the floor.

What was I doing? Why was I there? Why wasn't I in my own *cloakroom!*

As I tried to explain she turned me around and delivered a great whomping smack on my behind before sending me on my way her heckling tones still ringing in my ears.

I went back to my classroom with stinging cheeks, tears in eyes, and my little heart heavy. And believe me when I say this episode of injustice rankled for years.

So it was with no small relish that I recounted the story when we were having coffee in the staff-room one day, and it was worth it just to see her splutter! She didn't recall the incident, of course, and I couldn't resist a final dig when I asked with all wide-eyed innocence if such punishment was still requisite while I was there. Suffice to say I had the satisfaction of seeing her go bright red with the knowledge that this little dog did have its day..!

I was in my final year at school when unfortunately my family split up. As I'd always been one to champ at the institutional bit, it was with no small haste that I seized the opportunity to release myself from full-time education leaving a veritable cloud of dust in my wake! Independence was calling and I was all ears. With typical teenage aplomb I shook off any concerns anyone cared to make about future security and career prospects and sallied forth keen to make my own way in the world.

By this time I had moved to quite an affluent area of the city with my mother, and after placing an ad offering my babysitting services in the local shop, I soon found myself inundated by yummy-mummy's and plummy-poshies keen to make use of my services. Having come from a cosmopolitan neighbourhood (this translates roughly as 'the streets'!) and accustomed to a more humble clientele, I was quite taken aback at the differences I found in this brand new world and in *every* way!

The names for starters; Dominic's and Annabel's, Conrad's and Cuthberts'! Children so cosseted and well-scrubbed they oozed class and sophistication as they gazed upon me with an aura of confident bonhomie. I was agog. I had no idea such children existed! They were like little adults, and at times I would feel myself shrink in the face of such polished self-assurance as I would be commanded in ringing tones to read the story *again!*

But then you have to understand that I was used to the kind of children who generally ran riot, climbed trees, got dirty and played in back lanes, They were for the most part, loud, lively and charmingly cheeky, with names such as Sian and Paul, Susan and Dylan. And let's not forget the more diverse members of the community who had had cause to call upon my services.

Like sweet little Mohammed whose parents were from Iran. An only child and so painfully shy he would never speak in my presence. Indeed direct communication would take the form of a twitch of an eyebrow, or a widening of the pupil. He had the most beautiful dark brown eyes, and where his mouth wouldn't speak his eyes did and so we managed –

just!

Then there was the gaggle of delightful Iraqi sisters who would chatter incessantly and screech gleefully at my attempts to master their tongue. They were an absolute hothouse of blooming beauties, and I have particular warm memories of being invited to tea and sitting cross-legged on the floor as the mother cooked flat breads on a mini-stove. My first encounter with a Muslim family and in hindsight their hospitality was incredible in view of the fact I was a Westernized girl not yet sixteen.

But I guess I must have had the McPhee factor in bucketloads because I went then from ordinary back-street babysitter to Nanny of Neverland – at least that was how it seemed at the time. Large posh houses with wall to wall carpets; all mod-cons, three or more cars on the drive and full length fridges simply *bursting* with food!

I was in heaven!

Soon I was juggling jobs and parents with no small panache as weekend slots were in high demand so compromise on all fronts was called for. Even an extra fiver waved before my eyes would not induce me to part ways with a prior arrangement and I always, always stuck to the script.

Integrity is everything if you want people to ask you back – especially when you enjoyed *carte blanche* with the entire contents of the larder!

The most memorable family I worked for offered me a golden ticket to move away with them to a large rural property where I would have my own accommodation. No big deal, you're thinking, but for the fact I could also bring my horse! That in itself is no mean offer, and it was one of those times in your life when you just *know* a path waits with all manner of opportunities, but having recently become engaged, I declined.

The engagement didn't work out and I would often look

back and wonder how life would've shaped u if I'd thrown X
in my lot with Denzel and Dominic. This particular train of
thought arises every time I hear a song from 'Fiddler on the
Roof' and immediately I'm transported back to their living
room. This wonderful old classic was the only film available
to anyone in the house above the age of five and I watched it
religiously on rainy days when the children took their nap.
The family had a video recorder and a VHS, no less! That, in
my day, was like having an all-dancing all-singing home
cinema complete with popcorn and sweeping curtains - just
being able to sit back and lose yourself in a film without all
the adverts was a joy in itself. Suffice to say I remember
most of the lyrics after thirty five years and can still sing
along with a lusty croak. Sadly, however, my hips no longer
allow me the pleasure of re-enacting the Russian foot-crawl
in the Tavern scene and perhaps I should be grateful for
that...

Another family I will never forget was also another very
nice Jewish couple who lived in a lovely big house on the
suburbs of town, and I remember them particularly for two
reasons. The first, was for the tomatoes – yes you read that
right; tomatoes. And this was because they weren't just *any*
tomatoes, these were from a high-end supermarket and I had
never tasted the like before or since. They were absolutely
delicious!
Now I'm a bit of a serial grazer once I set my taste buds on
something, so as they duly stocked up on tomatoes and
mayonnaise, these sandwiches became my daily fare. I never
however, dared touch the sweetie jar that had all of the
mystique of the Kabbalah. It was a large and ornate and sat
tantalisingly high on a shelf like some holy relic. This
receptacle was the domain of the mother and the mother
only. It came out (although I never saw it) when she deemed

the behaviour of her children worthy of a treat.

For someone with such a raging sweet-tooth as I, this house-rule was akin to torture. But I'd convinced myself that every wrapped goodie was probably accounted for, so I'd just gaze longingly when the sugar levels dropped and wonder how the kids didn't slowly go mad.

The other lasting memory was the fact that they didn't celebrate Christmas, and as I was working for them during this period, this troubled me greatly, being still new to the bigger world around me and different religious beliefs.

I didn't live in on this job and when I'd commute – on foot, of course! (Shank's Pony is the only way to get about when you're poor and living on peanuts) I'd pass all of the houses with their sparkly big trees as they filled the bay windows - then when I'd get to their house and there would be nothing and my heart would droop.

When I'd take the two boys down to the park to feed the ducks, all tucked up in their woollies looking like wise little men – and I have to say they were the most well-behaved and earnest little children I had ever known – they wouldn't so much as bat an eyelid at the glittery displays of as we walked past. I found this indifference troubling and as Christmas was coming I also found myself in something of a dilemma.

I wanted to buy a present for the boys. Nothing major, just a token gift, but I was concerned such an act might cause offence. Mum was strait-laced and strict, the father even more so, yet it didn't feel *right* not to give them *something*! This became massive for me and I dilly-dallied until I finally came to a decision. Throwing caution to the wind I bought them each a selection box because if the worst came to the worst they would not go to waste!

On the appointed day and my last shift before Christmas, it was with no small feeling of trepidation that I offered my gifts to the mother and braced myself for her reaction. But she surprised me.

Not only did the usually stiff features soften, but she genuinely seemed touched and thanked me with sincerity. She then surprised me further by slipping a small gift into my hands as I was leaving with muted greetings for the season. I remember walking home that day with a spring in my step suffused with the spirit of Christmas and with all the joy of a fiddler on the roof!

I have to say that I was very lucky with the children I looked after. No major drama's but there has been the odd tricky moment, like the time I went for an interview and the father turned out to be a local builder who would wolf-whistle every time I walked past the site. That was pretty awkward especially in view of the fact his wife was as lovely as she was unsuspecting of her husband's leeriness at work – as she was of my rather fruity rejoinders that a sailor would be proud of.

Yep, that was a bit of a sticky one, but more especially for him as he squirmed before me in fear of what I might say. I simply enjoyed the moment and went on to blithely look after their delightful daughter, as he, lesson learned (I hope!), went on to treat me with maximum respect.

Parents could be very generous and the relationship between child-carer and employer would often depend on the disposition of the latter. Sometimes I would be treated like one of the family, other times little more than the paid help. It's a fine line and not always an easy one. I can remember having my first taste of gin with one mum when she insisted we share a festive tipple – the fact I was just one year shy of the legal age was irrelevant, but I stopped after three and made my excuses as her eyes began to glaze and marital woes fell from her lips. Rule of thumb: never get involved with the 'domestics' and besides, a girl fresh out of school is hardly marriage guidance material!

But for the most part, bathroom sets and boxes of chocolates were the norm, with the occasional cash bonus if you were lucky. Looking after other peoples' children definitely paid, but as I grew older I realised that there was more ways of earning a crust than singing 'The wheels of the bus...' and wrangling smelly nappies.

By the time I reached eighteen I realised that it was time for this particular Mary Poppins to unfurl her umbrella and set off in search of horizons new. It was good while it lasted, and I had the pleasure of knowing some really lovely families, but my feet were itching and little did I know that my life ahead would be dictated by this itch and the desire to go with it. So there ended my brief but rewarding career in child-care as I ventured forth to sample the delights of waiting on tables and a whole new world of a life in service.

WENCH OR WAITRESS

For anyone who has never waited on table let me tell you
that there are requirements to do this job that would not be
out of place in the Diplomatic Service or undercover
operations! Waiters and waitresses work extremely hard as
they labour on the whim of Joe Public and often for very
little thanks. Along with the cleaners and the kitchen porters,
they are the unsung heroes of the 'Hotel World' so that we,
the customer, can sit back and be waited on hand and foot.
This I found out the hard way when I started my first job at a
newly-opened restaurant in the centre of town. As I donned
the apron for the first time little did I know what I was
letting myself in for...

It was an American style diner that served massive burgers,
humungous steaks and mountains of fries. They also did
fancy cocktails and colossal desserts that all but screamed
with the calories.

Having only ever eaten out and had chicken and chips in a
basket this was quite an eye-opener for me, but it was the
behaviour of my new employers that opened my eyes even
further and not in a nice way!

The restaurant was the baby of three local businessmen

whose people-skills were on a par with Genghis Khan. For someone fresh from the cosy confines of family life in suburbia, their style of management was a brutal awakening and I reeled before it.

Long hours, loud music, trying to raise a smile after six hours on your feet with no break, and it was busy, relentless, hair-raising and hot - and that was just dealing with the three bosses who liked to take a hands-on approach in every way! I don't have much recall about the customers, other than their whoops and gasps of awe as you placed the laden plates before them – I do, however, remember my employers *very* well.

When you're young and have had limited contact with the concrete world that is the jungle, to suddenly find yourself amidst a pack of wily old predators comes, understandably, as something of a shock, and working for these three beasties was no exception.

They were my first introduction to the worst kind of employer in what should have been a modern working life in a modern working world. But for them, the passing of a century evidently meant nothing as Victorian Values were employed with all the gusto of Bumble the Beadle in Oliver Twist!

Amigo Number One was Front of House and did so with all of the acidity of 'Blackadder'. Most memorable was his lop-sided smile that was more of a smirk and a sure sign he was pissed off. He'd mince about the tables hissing orders his eyes throwing daggers if you so much as got an order wrong. To the customers he was so obsequious it was a wonder he never disappeared up his own arse! I have never before, or since, met an individual so constantly on the verge of an all-out tantrum, and at the first sign of that curling lip we would scuttle nervously before him in fear of our lives!

Then there was Amigo Number Two who was probably the

least obnoxious of the three for the fact he wasn't the
brightest. Big, beefy, there was a distinct troll-look about
him (please refer to the LOTR'S) or for a more in-depth
insight, The Hobbit) and his domain was the bar.
Incongruously squeezed into a bright Hawaiian shirt, he
would shuffle back and forth stirring and shaking with a
bovine look of happiness on his face. I think this was due in
two parts; firstly he got to partake of the various beverages,
and judging by his high colour he did this frequently- and
secondly, the Elizabeth Taylor look-alike.
This ol' glamour-puss could often be found perched at the
bar as a steady stream of free drinks went her way.
I never really figured out who she was; a silent partner who
drank all the profits or a lady-of-the night enjoying a break.
Either way, I lost count of the times I'd glance across
enviously and wish for just five minutes on that stool and for
her to don my apron and feel the heat as the hair frizzled and
the mascara melted.
So as Richard- Burton-wannabe Amigo Number Two served
cocktails and ogled the lovely 'Liz', getting his attention
could be tricky as he treated each drinks order as an
interruption. Small wonder the business went bust.
And lastly we come to the jewel in the crown; Amigo
Number Three. Ahhh... Amigo Number Three. Patron chef
and 'Chief Groper' with a propensity to swig endless halves
of lager as he sweated like a pig on a stick over the grill.
Fleshy, jowly, flamboyant to the point of foppish - he had a
penchant for flirting with anything that didn't have a dick
and was the epitome of sexual predator.
Indisputably the alpha-male of the pack, he was the only one
who had the audacity to grab and fondle at any given
opportunity. His particular favourite was to undo your bra-
strap when you weren't looking before guffawing as you
scrambled to redress yourself in horror before the customers

noticed. Not always an easy task when you've a plate full of food in both hands...

Such behaviour was the norm in this hot hellish hole of an eatery. And as you'd fend off yet another attack by a great greasy paw it soon became apparent that a certain form of body contortion came naturally but there was always fear in your heart.

Ironically at the end of the shift, when the last customer had weaved out into the night and 'Liz' had vacated the bar. Serial-groper Amigo Number Three would come over all fatherly and insist on feeding you. This 'nourishment' took the form of a great burger practically forced down your neck. I believe this compensation for running you ragged for hours without a break, but after juggling hot plates of food all night the last thing you wanted to do was eat it.

Have you ever tried to operate with an excruciating belly-ache with enough gas in it to raise the Titanic? I'm talking about a stomach so full of wind you could run an orchestra - because it's not just *any* old wind, it's *trapped wind!* Caused by stress and sneaky sausage-fingers forever grappling at your underwear.

I don't mean to sound ungrateful, but being made to sit down to stodge of fried food when you're well past the hunger game is akin to a special kind of torture. All you want to do is get the hell out of *Dodge,* but to keep the peace, and because a huge plate has been dumped in front of you cooperation is the better part of valour.

Gamely chewing on a lump of charred anus whilst trying to ignore the pain is further exacerbated when a cold fizzy drink is thrust in your face with the instruction to 'drink up because you must be thirsty'!

This dining experience was a debacle and will no doubt live with me forever. Feet aching, eyes burning, back groaning breasts all but shrunk with the indignation of earlier assaults, release when it came, was sweet. As the waiting-staff made a mad scramble for the door I'd stagger out to a waiting taxi completely attuned to how Moses must have felt when he shook off the sands of Egypt...

I look back now and see it for what it was. A nightmare on every level and how I'd imagine being submerged in *Dante's* equivalent of dining hell as your soul burnt slowly to a crisp. Besides, having my bra twanged every five minutes like it was a national sport, such treatment was not conducive to my sense of self-worth, nor was the paltry pound an hour they paid for the privilege! Something had to give and it wasn't going to be my bra strap - not anymore. So I delivered my notice – or in this case, a distinct lack of. It was my *coupe de grace*.

As anyone who works in hospitality knows, Saturday nights are the busiest times, the holy of holies, not the time to pull a sickie, and definitely not the time to quit. Knowing this I timed my phone call perfectly – just after six when Amigo Number Three would be firing up the ovens already having his first lager of the night. Amigo Number Two squeezed into yet another ridiculous shirt as he waited like a love-sick fool for the lovely 'Liz'.

And Amigo Number One, as I knew, would already be pacing as he practised the lip-curl in anticipation of playing the tyrant. So when the phone rang with the news that a member of staff will not be coming in, you can safely assume that there will be something of a hostile reaction. Add on the fact that this particular staff member will not be coming back – ever – and you have the difference between a yowling cat and a roaring lion.

So suffice to say, it was with no small pleasure when I hung up on Amigo Number One as his voice screeched to a pitch I didn't think possible. And I walked away vowing never to be so harangued and humiliated again.

It was many years before I donned the apron again and understandably I was a bit nervous, until I realised that my first experience was an exceptional one. It was do-able and bearable as long as you had oodles of patience and a good sense of humour.

The last part is particularly important because there will always be people who'll look down their nose at you when you wait-on. They might be the nicest, most amenable and *reasonable* folk outside of a restaurant - but as soon as you put a napkin on their lap they can undergo a complete personality change and become the diners from hell! They'll tut, they'll sigh, they'll roll their eyes and mutter with displeasure as you scurry about avidly trying to please the unappeasable. What makes it worse, of course, is knowing that your efforts will all be for nothing because they'd sooner starve and eat the napkin than say thank you and leave a tip.

The only way to deal with the dissatisfied diner is to ensure service is exceptionally pleasant and give lots of eye-contact. The latter will usually make them pull their necks in for shame. For how can you rail against somebody when they're so clearly doing their best?

It won't always work of course, but I would just pretend I was in a sitcom or a scene from a soap opera and enact my role. This used to work for me and would help ease the inevitable chagrin when your efforts were so poorly rewarded.

Small comfort could be taken afterwards when the last table was cleared and staff would sit down and relax with a drink or two. These times were the best, the most precious, the most underestimated moments of sheer joy. End of shift, when you finally got to put your feet up and compare notes; marvelling that someone didn't get their soup in their lap, the hair that was spotted - but too late, the misunderstanding over the bill that culminated in the manager being called and a grilling on the spot because the customer, surely, could never have got it so wrong!

It helps to have the skills of a United Nations Diplomat when you wait on table; the patience of Job, and a readiness to switch from grinning idiot to gurning concern when something's not right. The ability to adopt a whole medley of facial expressions also comes in handy when some diners go through the menu like it's an exam of life-changing proportions.

They can't decide between the pork and the fish because the stuffed medallions will give them a restless night, and the seabass, flatulence. But they don't really fancy anything else, so you stand there pen poised over the pad as other diners glare and demand attention as though you're the one to blame for such procrastination.

Inwardly you just pray at this point the questions don't start because this will then confirm that the dithering diner either;

a) doesn't get out much

b) is showing off in front of their dining party (or God forbid, the whole table!)

Or

c) knows exactly what they are doing and take a delight in holding you to ransom as they nit-pick their way through the entire menu with a smirk on their lips.

It is frustrating, futile, and frequently unnecessary. But what can you do? You try to pull away with the breezy assurance you'll be back as soon as they've decided, then a hand reaches out and all but arrests you.

You look back and find you are pinned.

"I haven't finished yet!"

You give a sickly smile; you are well and truly trapped. The onslaught begins...

What kind of potatoes are in the *Dauphinoise*?
How long has the meat been hanging?
Are the herbs in the sauce freshly chopped or dried?
Why aren't there any chips on the menu?
Or as one woman memorably piped up, 'I don't like garden peas. Have you any mushy?'
I could go on.
Fortunately, sanity is spared by the nice customers, the *easy* customers, the kind of *clientele* that makes doing your job a pleasure. When service is over you part ways with a warm glow inside because the business of dining out couldn't have gone more smoothly. A happy customer means you've done your job properly – and with your bra still intact by the end of it!

I have fond memories of my time at a well-known golf club but for probably all the wrong reasons. Here the whole success of the day would depend upon the toastiness of a teacake, the crispiness of the bacon, or with some regulars, the alacrity of your service. It soon became apparent that in the golfing fraternity there are foibles and rituals that must be adhered to in the endless quest for a hole in one. To say they bemused me is beyond measure.
For the most part expectations were genteel and relatively mundane and the tips so good you'd do an Irish jig with a tray of coffees on your head if the occasion demanded it. Overall the clubhouse had an ambience that was both homely and pleasing, and I was quite taken with this new world of plus-fours and those willing to stomp the fairways in all kinds of weather. There was something almost old-fashioned about it all, the menfolk in particular and I looked upon their fraternity with an indulgent, kindly eye – until I met the 'Lady-golfers'!
In the famous opening words of Jane Austen's classic 'Pride

and Prejudice', she begins with the lines; 'It is a universally acknowledged truth that...' *It is a truth universally a...* +
Well, in this case, allow me the first part to go on and say '...that, there are certain kinds of women who detest other women, and will make it their life's work to denigrate their own species at any given opportunity.'
Should you also have the added disadvantage of being seen as inferior in any way, then don a pinny with a long-suffering look and watch the She-Wolves go!
Seem a bit harsh? Yes, it is. Having to deal with the hostility of one wolf was bad enough – but when they were all together, Oh Lordy, it was like being bought to bay by the whole pack!
Not an encounter for the faint-hearted - their snapping jaws could puncture your shield of self-worth within seconds!
And so what does this entail, I hear you ask?
Ok. Picture the scene; the bell sounds in the kitchen and out you sail, all wreathed in smiles only to be met by a cluster of older women who then pointedly ignore you in between the odd glance of contempt.
Resisting the urge to hop like a child from one foot to the other, you hover uncertainly, your pad and pen poised as you try to disguise your growing discomfort with a smile usually seen on the face of the condemned man (or woman!).
They chatter on. You wait. They talk some more and still you wait, until finally you give a polite little clearing sound in the back of your throat, and that gets their attention!
They stop and they glare; in situ, like a well-rehearsed *Why? +*
'Haka' of the eyes as the silence draws out between you.
Your stomach starts to churn as you realise in another universally acknowledged truth that it is not for *you* to initiate the next part of the proceedings - it is for *them*! You also realise in that moment that if whipping the menial was still legal in this country you would be flung down and

treated to forty of the best.

There then follows the stand-off as you wither slowly beneath the collective glare of these menopausal Medusa's until the Alpha female addresses you in her best bark. This is swiftly followed through by the rest of the pack as they impart their orders with such speed you can barely keep up, and as the pen wiggles furiously across the pad and you just *know* that they're doing it deliberately. But better to fall on your sword than show any incompetence, yet there's a problem.

You're not sure about one or two of the orders and have to double- check. Better to feel the wrath now than after if Harriet doesn't get her cappuccino, or God forbid, you serve Lemon Meringue instead of the Lemon Drizzle!

You pause, you swallow, you then shift your feet because by now the orders have been despatched and you are dismissed; ignored; no longer visible and almost certain to invite a furious fuselage of snarling from the pack should you dare interrupt again.

But there's nothing else for it and out comes the tiniest cough and this time there is a surge of hormonal aggression as each one throws themselves around, and you just *know* you're on the cusp of being brought down by the pack!

The Alpha glares at you, lips curling before snapping, *'Yes, what is it?'*

As you stutter your way through your request for further clarification, you feel the eyes of the rest of the clubhouse on your back as this public mauling unfolds like an over-acted Greek tragedy. There is some comfort to be gained amidst the frostiness of your treatment as some of the more kindly male clientele emit a steady stream of warm sympathy in your direction. But this is women's business in its nastiest form and they knew well to keep out of it.

So what do you do when faced with such exploits that

wouldn't look out of place within the killing ground of a Roman Amphitheatre? Who do you turn to when even the Stewardess runs the daily gauntlet of an ever-threatening 'thumbs-down'? And the Steward, who looks in fear of his life should they so much as even glance his way as he sidles past with the look of an ear-marked rabbit!

There is only one way to deal with these kinds of people and that's to give 'em sugar - and plenty of it.

No other way, wile, or weaponry would've touched the self-assurance of this particular pack; you could have curtsied, self-flagellated before them or simply crawled across the floor - and still they would have stepped over you as you were berated for not doing more.

Now, it is *another* universally acknowledged truth that those who dole out unkindness can rarely take it when it's been recycled and sweetly delivered back. They throw you a cactus; you hand them a rose. They spike you with vitriol; you ooze compassion. They hector, they bicker, you lean down and gaze into those bitter faces and smile serenely as though the acidity of their remarks are nothing more than a language of love you don't understand. Then watch as their eyes flicker and look away, the rigid lines of their face become slack because they can't keep it up; they just can't, and then know in that instant you've won!

It took a few good doses of sugar before I gained their respect, albeit grudgingly and not without the occasional growl. But customer relations improved sufficiently to make future service less daunting and we rubbed along like silk and sandpaper after that.

Fortunately I never ran across such a hybrid mix of female powerful personalities again but it was a good learning curve, and some years later I actually bumped into the Alpha female at local event who was sweetness itself. Proof that power often lies in the pack...

It soon became apparent to me, however, that although I generally enjoyed the interaction that comes with customer service, waiting on table whilst doubling as the whipping boy was definitely not for me.

I found bar-tending much more amenable as contact, for the most part, could be fleeting and impersonal with the added benefit of a block of wood between you and the punters. But life in the hospitality industry has no time for such indulgences, and if all hands were required to the deck; out came the pinny and the rictus smile as you piled the plates along your arm and got on with the job.

Such an instance occurred when I was supervisor at a very nice hotel. The boss had failed to adjust the rota and put the call out to all staff for a sumptuous and very large charity dinner. With a skeleton crew of just six – including Chef, his Sous and the pot-washer; the other hapless three were left to wait on one hundred and twenty diners, this being yours truly and the two proprietors.

It was one of those occasions in life when you truly feel murder in your heart. There is incompetence and then there is crass incompetence. The hour is upon you and inwardly you dither on the verge of walking out. You just *know* you're about to enter a nightmare that will go on for hours. But common decency stays the desire to stomp and you reconcile yourself to a night's hard graft.

The front desk is abandoned and the answer-phone switched on as guests begin to arrive, You smile and you simper whilst showing them to their seats and then begins the dreaded mantra; 'I'm so sorry, but I'm afraid service will be a little slow tonight as we're short staffed, but we'll do our very best not to keep you waiting too long between courses.' You murmur this repeatedly as you usher and nod. The trick is to convey a sense of controlled calm, as if such a mishap is of no great inconvenience. But it is a carefully cultivated front to hide the fear in your eyes, for there are few things worse than a belligerent diner with an empty belly!

Nobody seems to be really listening. You are like the Ghost of Christmas Past, the Invisible Woman, barely-observed as your bleats go unacknowledged, and at this point, unchallenged. Nobody is really listening because a night of food, wine and convivial company lies ahead.

Everyone is happy. You are aware that this is a yearly event and that all attendee's have probably been looking forward to it for months – as you are that this is the first time *we* are hosting and will probably be the last!

It is like a doomed ship all set to run aground – and there is absolutely nothing you can do about it than grab on to a life-jacket and hang on!

Thankfully, the house wine is already uncorked and sat waiting on the tables. As you make your escape to the kitchen, you take heart and rally for the task ahead - because everything has been pre-ordered and nothing can go wrong, right?

Wrong.

As you scurry madly between the kitchen and a sea of hungry watchful eyes, the litany of complaints begins.

'I ordered the soup. Why have I got pate? I don't even *like* pate!'

'Sorry, my dear, but I'm *sure* I ordered the melon...'

'What's *this? I didn't order this!'*

You grimace, you gurn, the sweat breaks out as the muttering reaches a babble and there's a definitive change in the mood. The wine has kicked in and people who would normally be mild-mannered change into petulant children because they didn't want white rolls they wanted *brown*! Why isn't there enough staff? How come he's got more sauce than *I have!*

Cue the next part of your performance as you juggle plates and awkward questions; absorb copious amounts of humble pie interspersed with moments of humour. If you want to make it out of the building in one piece, then an appeal to the better nature of the customer is required. In desperation you offer a silent prayer. Somehow you *must* get them on-side!

Quips about *Fawlty Towers* and the fact there is a full moon pending raises a few eyebrows as you wheel and witter like some culinary court jester. All pretence of professionalism is now well and truly down the pan because they know as well as you do that the whole gig is a complete disaster!

There's only one way to go as the wine, thankfully, does its job in another way, and they begin to see the funny side. They join in swapping plates as finally they find enough sympathy in their hearts to rally to a lost cause. And all the while you chunter quietly in your head as you devise all forms of revenge you will visit on the boss as he strides about with a fixed grin you'd pay a king's ransom to wipe off!

Because it isn't just the front of house you have to deal with, it's also the mood in the kitchen, and the heat has been steadily rising as Chef is on the verge of an apoplectic fit. He grumbles and he curses, he glowers and he snarls and all you can do is keep your head down and try not to draw the feverish eye.

We wait in respectful silence like mourners at a wake as lamb shank is slapped on plates, pork medallions flung into place. The Sous Chef, sweating as much from stress as he is from the ovens, hovers nervously as he plops a portion of *dauphinoise* on one plate, a splodge of mash on another. The air is tight, the tension palpable. Everyone wants to kill the boss and I'm reminded of that notorious chant from the classic, 'Lord of the Flies' - *'Kill the pig!' Kill the Pig!'* that seems to resonate around the kitchen like a silent mantra but we need to get the mains out first.

The second marathon now takes place as you scurry back and fore with as many plates as you can carry including all the side orders of veg. Plates are hot and the metal receptacles even hotter, but there's no time to do anything other than wince as you dream of ice and a cold running tap. Someone wants extra *jus* for the lamb and you gulp loudly in anticipation of putting this forward to the ravening chef who is still plating up. Not the best time; so you nod and smile and hope once they tuck in they'll forget, but there's a hand waving furiously and someone is calling *'Ju! Ju!'*

You grind your teeth before baring them in a tight-faced grimace. For God's sake, don't they realise that if you go in and ask for extra sauce the chances are you're not likely to come back out!?? That to interrupt the flow of service at this point would be akin to suicide of the most machoistic kind and probably with a machete! Indeed at this juncture the prospect of simply walking into Mordor would be far more appealing.

But do they care? Oh no! This leads me to believe that not one diner in the history of food and beverage would even stop to consider the fine line that is walked between serving staff and chefs. How the former often brave the machete and the knife as they put their life on the line for the sake of some extra gravy!

Chefs are the Krakens of the Kitchen! The Ogres of the Ovens! An omniscient presence of such undiluted power you must tread, as on egg-shells, only speak, when you are spoken to, commence service, when you are told to. Try not to flinch before tantrums of tsunamic proportions engulf the kitchen as soufflés flop and brandy snaps crumble – and should there even be anything so much of a *whisper* of complaint from table - then best take to your heels and run. You bounce nervously with the unspoken request like a lozenge still sat on your tongue until something transmits, and then the feverish eye is upon you.

Like some ridiculous cartoon-character your lips stretch impossibly wide as you break into the kind of smile that screams *Asylum!* You're now actually starting to bob up and down and you can't stop it, for a frown has now creased the chef's harassed brow and you know you have your moment, you *have* to do it you *must* make the request!

The customer is waiting and now everyone has stopped what they are doing and are watching the scene unfold with a kind of anticipatory dread.

"*Jus,*" you squeak.

"*WHAT?*"

You clear your throat nervously and the frown deepens.

"*Jus*, a customer has asked for some more... *jus*..."

You trail off miserably as the frown now becomes a fully-fledged scowl. There follows a long silence. Everyone is frozen into place as for the first time in your life you empathise completely with the bleating waif in 'Oliver' who has dared to ask for 'more.'

"*Jus?*" The word is spat like it's some kind of blasphemy and you nod timidly wishing for the floor to swallow you up. With a dramatic air worthy of a great Shakespearian moment Chef gestures to the Sous who flutters uncertainly and he barks, "Well you heard the girl, *get more jus!*" and then under his breath so the boss doesn't hear, but of course he does, '*F*cking customers!*'

Inwardly you draw a deep breath and grab the proffered jug like it's the Holy Grail before re-entering the restaurant with a slight swagger. You faced the beast and survived!

Main course over and what feels akin to having run a second

marathon, there now follows a third as you clear down
before taking out the desserts. The home-run is finally in
sight and you put on a spurt.

Cue the dramatic tune from 'Chariots of Fire' as you lurch
gamely back and fore with tiramisu in one hand fruit
meringue in the other. There's a light in your eyes and a
flame of enthusiasm that even a demand for extra custard
cannot put out.

 We are, ladies and gentlemen, now at the arse-end of
service. Everything will now begin to calm down. Chef will
undergo a miraculous personality change and the world will
turn back on its head.

As the kitchen winds down and the ovens are switched off,
there then follows the mass clean-up as the dishes keep
coming and somewhere, in the back, amidst a sea of soap
suds is the second most important person in the culinary set-
up; the kitchen porter.

Any good waiting-on personage worth their salt will always
get stuck in and help out at the sink for there are few things
more sad than seeing a lonesome figure gradually being cut
off by a rising tide of dishes. But not yet, as it's time to
clear down again and you suppress all feelings of guilt as the
poor sod disappears completely behind a wall of steam, for
now comes the requisite after-dinner coffees and *petit* fours.
The latter, which must be presented nicely on a tiny plate
atop a snowy-white doily all but get lobbed onto a dish,
because frankly, at this point you are on the verge of
complete collapse and does anyone notice? No. The end of
the evening is nigh. The food has been eaten. The wine has
been drunk. The mood is decidedly mellow and you dare to
anticipate a good tip.

You've run your arse off, after all. You've all but broken the
world record for sheer tenacity and *panache* as you've
grappled and giggled, schmoozed and suffered all manner of

indignities in the name of customer service, right?
Wrong.
On this most memorable of occasions there wasn't so much
as a sou or a shilling, not even a jingle of shrapnel left in
acknowledgement of my efforts. With an almost sense of
disbelief you watch as each guest wends their way out as
you echo 'Goodnight' like a demented parrot. And no, I
don't mind confessing I inwardly cursed each one and
wished them indigestion!
The last guest finally departed, you return to the kitchen
with a new-found stomp in your step. There's still the
business of the boss, and although the urge to pick him up
and throw him bodily has now passed due to extreme
physical exhaustion, there's still fire enough in your belly to
give him a bit of 'what-for'.
The wind is well and truly shaken out of your war-sails as he
comes towards you with something cold and fizzy. Your
capitulation is instant and complete. With a mouth so
parched your tongue feels like a strip of leather the sight of
that molten-gold glass being thrust before you is like manna
from heaven. You accept it graciously with a murmur of
thanks. It is an unprecedented gesture and you know it's his
way of saying sorry.
You look around and see only appeased faces as they suck
upon their bubbling flutes and know a truce is in place and
there will be no killing of any pigs tonight.
The mood becomes mellow and everyone mucks in because
common decency demands it. It is what bonds us and keeps
us together as a team. Even Chef has lightened up courtesy
of the fizz and is wielding a tea towel. I crack a joke about
the *jus*; he waves a hand and is human again. The chatter
goes on as we post-mortem the night. The customers, the
complaints, the sight of someone staggering into the wrong
toilet trying not to cringe as one brave soul warbled

'Delilah'.

Nothing is spared, no detail goes unreported as we all share anecdotes and giggle at the ridiculous. The boss starts to lose his slightly harried look as he realises he's safe and that perhaps he didn't need to dry the cutlery after all. The one job we all hate, but he volunteered as much to have *carte blanche* of anything sharp as much as anything else – and slowly but surely the end is in sight then the last dish is put away.

We all smile at each other in a goofy kind of way. We did it. We made it through. And as we all traipse out quietly into the night and home to our beds, it is with a sense of achievement not unlike that of the broken-backed slave when the last stone capped the pyramids.

As a footnote to this particular establishment, that was, to be fair, one of the nicest places I'd ever worked in and it's worth sharing an anecdote of the two hundred pound bottle of wine. In the few years I worked there I was fascinated (albeit agog might be a better word) as was everyone else by this mystical, almost mythological mega-expensive bottle of plonk! We just couldn't comprehend it, relate to it, fathom out why on earth anyone could set such a high price on six glasses at just under forty quid a shot - never mind fork out for it.

We were bemused, bewildered, and not a little in contempt for such blatant extravagance, so imagine our surprise when a couple ordered a bottle, not just once, but *twice* during the two nights they were staying.

This was an event! And it became even more so when they kindly (deliberately?) left a glassful in the bottle at the end of each night. This unprecedented act saw us in a flurry of excitement - at last we were going to be able to taste the fabled wine for ourselves.

It was a momentous occasion!

There is a scene in Charles Dickens's 'A Christmas Carol' when Mrs Cratchet comes out from the scullery with the highlight of the family's humble dinner. But whereas she had a frugal Christmas pud on a plate, here was I with the dregs of an expensive bottle of wine that sat waiting at the bottom. The air of revered anticipation, however, was much the same and we simply gazed at it for some moments before I poured it out. The moment had arrived. There was the pause of all pauses as I, as befitted my position as hotel supervisor, took the first sip.

And wrinkled my nose.

The rest of the staff gave a collective 'Coo' because they weren't expecting that, indeed *I* was expecting that! So I took another and furrowed my brow. I then turned to the kitchen porter and proffered the glass. It is my belief that these unsung heroes of the kitchen are often overlooked and besides, when would he ever get an opportunity to sample something so ostentatious?

His eyes were unusually bright as he took the glass with a reverence normally seen in a communion service, and after taking a small sip he too, pulled a face and looked askance. It would be fair to say that by the time this arse-end of wine had done the rounds the general consensus of opinion came in and it was unanimous; it wasn't actually anything special, if anything it was quite bland and so why on earth would anyone spend so much money on it?

We were most bemused. Perhaps our palates were too accustomed to cheap supermarket wine and simply uneducated in the appreciation of a good grape. Whatever the reasoning it was a defining moment in as much that *more* doesn't necessarily mean *better!* Our seemingly wasteful donators had actually bestowed on us a great kindness, because who, in their right mind, would leave a full glass of

a two hundred pound bottle of wine deliberately? Not just
once, but *twice!*

My rose-tinted theory (and I'm sticking to it) was that they
had money and kindness enough to share and let's be honest,
even if we'd all clubbed together to buy a bottle, the
disappointment would so have outweighed the treat factor
and we'd have felt well and truly cheated!

So my thanks to the mystery couple for their unwitting, or
otherwise, generosity, for we never regarded that particular
plonk with such unadulterated reverence again. Indeed we
continued to imbibe our Merlots and Rioja's for a fiver and   ✗
were most grateful for it!

Waiting on table is without doubt an excellent way of
learning how to deal with people and when to keep your
mouth shut. but it's also a little like a table-lottery because
you don't know what you'll get; whether it's complaints
aplenty, sweetness and light and or if you're lucky, a jolly
good tip!

Tips are the mainstay of the service industry; the added
perks, the anticipated treasure. And as the hospitality trade
is amongst the lowest paid, it is also for some, the difference
between butter on your bread or margarine that week.

One of the places I worked in enjoyed the most amazing
generosity from guests and it was my job to dole it out. As
an unspoken but expected rule, Head Chef is allocated the
highest amount, and then down the ranks to the lowly
kitchen porter. I have to admit I was never a fan of this
system because not all guests who tipped did so solely for
the food or for that matter, the service. In fact I was of the
mind that the tips were for *everyone* who pulled their
weight, and that they should be rewarded accordingly.

More than once the Head Chef and I butted heads when it
was discovered that the 'Pot-boy' had received almost as

much in his envelope as he did. But my argument was
always the same; stand for hours at a steaming sink and
you'll discover a fast appreciation of what a greasy sauna is
like, not to mention scrubbing saucepans when everyone else
has gone home!

No, I'm afraid that waitressing was not for me and being
elevated to *Maitre'd* was no less demanding – you just get to
deal with the bigger crap and become piggy in the middle.
The old adage that the customer is always right can often fall
at the first fence; it's hard not to argue when the customer is
so obviously wrong and I've never been a nodding dog.
Hence my next foray into another aspect of the service
industry as I stripped off my apron and tried out my talents
as a barmaid.

TIME PLEASE

Now back in my day, a bar person was regarded in only one of two ways. At the high end of the scale, a bar attendant would throw on a dickey bow, adopt a subservient manner and could expect at best to receive a grudging respect. There's something rather *panache* about making up a cocktail. A little flourish here, a glossy cherry there, the chink of ice and an olive or two. The defining moment when an exotic beverage is poured into a gleaming glass before being placed next to a dish of nuts and other unidentifiable nibbles!

This sublime imagery I had picked up, of course, from watching the *James Bond* films as a child and I thought it all looked wonderfully chic and glamorous.

The reality, however, was quite different. For a start, you were known as 'the barmaid' plain and simple. There were no such things as cocktails – at least not some of the places I worked and you'd have been laughed out of the bar if you'd asked for one! The only thing shaken was for last orders and 'nibbles' were usually great chunks of porky scratchings that could leave you, if you were unlucky, toothless by the end of the night.

So when I decided to try my hand at the pumps, it was to

embark on an extremely steep learning curve made worse by the fact I'd blagged to get the job. It was just a backstreet pub I grant you, but the brewery had spent a fortune on refurbishment and it wouldn't have looked out of place on a classy London Street. From the outside... This was my first impression but it didn't take long before the rose-tinted glasses came off. A pub is not that much different to a book cover and this particular establishment was no exception. Externally it might have looked like a grand Victorian pile, but inside the clientele were anything and it was here I learned pub-culture old-school and in style.

I had hoped to hide my complete ineptitude behind a breezy manner and bright smiles, but there is no fool like a young fool and then, of course, there were the mistakes; lots of mistakes...

Pub customers, I quickly discovered, are remarkably observant, and as many of them spend their time propping up the bar you are forever in their sights. So when you mess up, as I often did, there is absolutely, literally, nowhere to hide - as I found out the hard way.

It also soon became clear that there are few things as endearing as the relationship between a barmaid and the regulars. If you tick all the right boxes you are taken under the wing, cherished and protected with an almost propriety air, and God help anyone who disrespects you. You become their friend, their confidante, the fount of all wisdom when they've sank one too many and become maudlin and meaningful in a meaningless kind of way.

This was something I was to learn over time, but firstly I had to get to grips with the pumps and the measures, the prices and the pipes. Even trickier however was being the new kid on the block.

I suddenly found myself amidst an established order of older barmaids who greeted me with barely concealed contempt.

This was a disconcerting experience and not a good start and I trembled beneath their withering regard.

Now as we all know, in order to rub along in any job it's imperative you get on with your workmates, and I can honestly say that I never had more empathy with Daniel in the lion's den than I did during those first few weeks!

My first and ultimate sin was that I was younger, *much* younger. And if that wasn't offensive enough their senses were further inflamed by the fact my backside was drawing too much attention from the punters. It was too much to be borne. They rallied in rebellion and submitted a vigorous complaint to the management. *No more jeans!*

This new directive, when sheepishly communicated to me by my usually blustering ex-rugby player of a boss was equally embarrassing for us both. For me that my denim-clad posterior had become the subject of such high feeling, and for him, that he couldn't handle a scrum of his own staff. For want of a better expression he had simply rolled over and handed them the ball.

That was bad enough. But the alternative was even worse. Quite horrifying in fact, because this meant I had to wear a *skirt!!!*

Please note the THREE exclamation marks, for they convey, I hope fervently, my absolute aversion to wearing anything that did not sit snugly between my legs at that time!

I *hated* skirts; I abhorred them with a passion. To my mind skirts were the invention of a chauvinistic devil! School had been a torment with the draughts and the awkwardness, the self-conscious attempts to sit down and get up every morning in assembly. Simply having to walk around in one for five years of my life had been like a penance for someone as tom-boyish as me. I'd sooner have walked around in a hair shirt with a cilice round my neck than have endured the torture of having to wear a *skirt!*

The ultimatum duly delivered there was a long pause as he sat there gazing at me apologetically as I battled furiously with my demons within. But there wasn't really any choice. In fact there *was* no choice. Jeans or job; it really was as simple as that.

I gathered myself together with what little dignity I could muster and gave a small nod. Sentence had been passed and the jury had spoken; for the crime of having a pert backside, how do you plead? Guilty, m'lud! It was all arse-backwards (s'cuse the pun!) and such behaviour would never be allowed now. But back in the day there was no legislation to spare you from green-eyed barmaids with big butts and bad attitudes. It was a defining moment for me on two fronts. One; that I was going to comply, despite my inherent abhorrence to wearing anything without a crutch, and two, that employee's, even lowly barmaids, sometimes had status enough to wield a certain amount of power. I shelved the latter for something told me I might want to draw on the implications of this situation at a later date.

And so began my first job pulling pints and pandering to the peculiarities of petty-minded people. Once my posterior was safely encased there began a slight thaw as I was slowly accepted into the pernickety pride on the understanding I was still a young cub and barely tolerated.

Full acceptance was heralded some months later, however, when there was a complete cessation of elbows in the ribs and being pushed at the pumps. It had been a bruising and educational experience, but once the claws had been sheathed and the teeth drawn in, I was suddenly like a long-lost daughter and it was like the sun coming out!

This complete turnaround left me feeling extremely bemused and you could almost hear my toes give a collective sigh of relief and as my ribs expanded with freedom. But if I thought I was out of the woods, I had another thing coming...

Providing free and unwitting entertainment was a large part of my role once I stepped behind that bar, and you could all but see the regulars settle back with their pints in anticipation of a few hours amusement.

I soon became known as *Calamity Jane* because if anything was going to go wrong, it often did and to me in spectacular fashion.

Now I'm not going to be dishonest and claim mitigating circumstances, I will hold my hand up fair and square and declare I was absolutely useless. Having never worked a bar before – contrary to how I'd waxed lyrical in the interview – there was obviously more to it than I could dream of and the customers soon sussed me out!

'I'll have a pint of black and tan,' was one example, and I'd hover uncertainly with a worried look thinking, *Black and tan! Black and tan? What the **** is a black and tan!*

'Oh, and he'll have a Brown Top.'

Brown Top! What the....?

A stand-off would then ensue as my mind went into overdrive with various possibilities and they'd all but hold their breath watching me with unconcealed enjoyment. This was the pastime of the punter who had nothing else better to do than bait the barmaid, but they actually ended up being my best teachers once I got them onside.

'Someone wants half and half with a dash! Wassa?' I'd hiss in an urgent aside.

'Half lager, half bitter with a dash of lemonade.'

'Ok. Snakebite, someone's asking for a snakebite! *What is it?'*

And they'd roll their eyes before sniggering amongst themselves as once again I stumbled about in complete ignorance.

Well I can remember being shouted by my first customer as I poured him the wrong bitter.

'No, not that *shite!*' he bawled his eyes practically popping out of his head, *'The other one!'*

'Oh!' I squeaked, 'sorry, when you said a pint of bitter I thought you meant...'

"*What*!' the brow became thunderous, 'Are you *stupid! I wouldn't drink that piss if it was the last drink on earth!'*

Suitably admonished I shuffled along to the next pump aware that every eye in the bar was on me as my cheeks flamed scarlet and their chortling assaulted my ears. Suffice to say after such humiliation I always made sure to ask first. That was the first lesson. The second was that punters can get incredibly touchy about their beer – had I been pouring a pint of poison his reaction couldn't have been more vehement. Men and their beer – underestimate the relationship between them at your peril!

A rough beginning and it didn't get any better. Take the wine pumps for instance. The one for the white was so stiff you'd practically dislocate your shoulder manning it. The only way was to heave down hard and even then all you'd get was a dribble. What made it worse was that you were aware of your facial expression as you did so. Think extreme constipation, fart on the cusp of bursting out and you get the picture – not a good look for anyone, much less a young woman in front of a grinning audience.

And then there was the red.

As loose as the white was tight the pump was practically a live wire at the slightest touch and would emit an explosive blast at a rate of knots. So you treated it, naturally, with the greatest of caution. Unless you are busy talking, of course, and are so distracted that you pull – *hard* – on the wrong pump and then the worst case scenario happens.

A fountain of red hits the bottom of the glass and then shoots several feet up into the air only to come down in a rosy cascade all over me and the poor sod at the bar. This is most unfortunate because he has no legs.

He is also blind.

The first he knows about it is when he's literally drenched in cheap French wine and simply sits there looking like some poor sap caught up in a bloodbath.

There is a shocked silence before the room erupts into laughter as I stand there absolutely dripping and frozen to the spot.

Mortified doesn't cover it. My eyes are riveted on this poor man whose bald head now has a rosy gleam as red rivulets run down his face. His unseeing stare locked somewhere off into the distance as the scarlet spray finally settles around him.

He doesn't move. I continue to stare like a hare caught in the headlights. This man is seriously disabled and I've just drenched him in France's 'finest' so it's fair to say my life flashed before my eyes.

As the hoots died down I see a slight twitch pull at the corner of his gaping mouth. Then his unseeing gaze glides across to where I'm stood before him, my hand still holding the glass before the offending pump and I can barely breathe for dread.

His mouth opens further and then from it – thank the gods! - comes a rumble of mirth as his face creases and his shoulders shake and I slump with relief. As he guffaws with the punters I dab at him with bar towels. I really can't apologise enough but he's decided to see the funny side. *I haven't had so much fun in ages*, he tells me, *I just wish I could've seen* your *face!*

Ironically, this was my 'finest moment' putting all other *faux pas* in the shade. *Calamity Jane* had struck again and no one was going to let me forget it!

But like all back-street boozers it wasn't all fun in a bun - there were dark moments, too. Like the time some young woman came wandering into the lounge one day behaving very strangely. As it was still early on a week day I was able to leave the bar and go round to where she was sitting because I knew immediately that something was wrong. She watched my approach warily fully expecting me to tell her to leave – she hadn't ordered a drink, after all, but there was nothing threatening about her demeanour. She simply looked lost and I was intrigued.

I sat down on a stool and smiled at her then asked if she was ok.

No, she wasn't. Her mother has just died and she didn't know what to do.

There was a long pause as I absorbed this development. It was as unexpected as it was bizarre because people didn't usually wander into pubs and plonk themselves down on hearing of bereavement. Or did they?

I studied her and took in the sallow face heavy with sadness, the weary eyes and something I couldn't quite put my finger on. Her appearance was crumpled and shabby and she looked, for want of a better word, rough.

My heart filled with pity. It was a chilly day and for lack of being able to offer anything else other than kindness I asked if she'd like a hot chocolate.

'I have no money,' she said flatly.

'I wasn't planning on charging you. On the house.'

She regarded me with thinly-veiled suspicion before giving a small nod. I went off to the kitchen and soon returned with a steaming mug that she took from me tentatively. Her manner reminded me of a wild creature that found itself in unfamiliar surroundings, and after satisfying myself no one was waiting to be served in the bar; I resumed my place and waited.

As the hot chocolate did its work she appeared to loosen up and began to talk in what could only be described as a rambling manner.

There was definitely something not right here, and I watched her closely as she made some cryptic remarks that didn't make sense before she finally dropped the bombshell.

Instinct told me to remain calm and I kept my expression neutral for now she was watching *me* closely before adding, 'I've only told you because I feel I can trust you. You won't call the police, will you?'

I shook my head and forced a reassuring smile to my face before leaning forward and patting her hand.

'No, of course not.'

There was a shout from the bar.

'Stay here,' I said rising, 'I'll just serve this customer and I'll be right back.'

Leaving her sipping hot chocolate I slipped back behind the bar, my mind in a whirl. This was going to take some delicate handling and I wasn't really listening as I endured the whining complaint of being a neglectful barmaid.

Pint pulled and an absent-minded apology given I shot back to the lounge half expecting her to be gone, but she was still there and now half-slumped, her gaze vague and wandering. It was time to act.

How's about another hot chocolate or maybe you would like something to eat?'

My voice sounded normal, solicitous even, as I hovered over her.

She gave a small nod as a frothy bubble appeared at the corner of her mouth, and without further ado I went into the kitchen and grabbed a pasty before taking a deep breath and picking up the phone.

'What are you doing?' demanded the landlady, who was willing to turn a blind eye to hot chocolate but not a free pasty and a phone call.

'I'm calling the police.' I said calmly.

'What!'

No self-respecting landlord or landlady wants the law on their premises, not unless they're on a friendly visit, and there was obviously something in my demeanour that was flagging up a less than friendly situation out front. She paused chopping onions as I dialled 999.

'Why? What's happened? *What's going on?'* she demanded eyes bright behind her glasses.

'I've got a woman in the lounge who's taken an overdose, yes, police, please!'

Her jaw dropped.

'That isn't the worse of it she's also done a runner from a mental institution and oh, yes, hello, is that the police? You'll also need to send an ambulance!'

After passing over the details I replaced the phone and hurried from the kitchen leaving the landlady riveted to the spot her knife still held aloft.

Feeling like Judas I returned to the lounge and was greeted by a vague smile from the young woman. By now she was starting to look really out of it.

'You haven't told anyone, have you?' she slurred.

I placed the pasty on the table and had to look her right in the eye and find the lie, because if I didn't she'd be off, overdose or not. Besides, I felt a sense of responsibility for her, and without further ado found myself shaking my head, 'No, no, don't worry.'

She reached out and took a listless bite of the pasty and leaned back chewing slowly as she regarded me like a trustful child, and my heart quailed at my betrayal.

There was movement in the hall and before we knew it two

police officers stepped into the lounge. They were quick, I'll give them that and they had come in the back way via the kitchen. The landlady hovered behind them a tea towel having replaced the knife, her eyes huge behind her glasses. The young woman sat up and her face puckered.

'You promised!'

I moved away.

'I'm sorry.'

She turned to glare at me, her face stricken and I was assailed by a terrible feeling of guilt.

I looked at the police instead who had stepped forward removing their helmets as they did so.

'Hello Frances,' said one of them kindly and sat on a stool, 'we've been looking all over for you.'

I dared to look back at the young woman who had now slumped back in her seat and felt a pang as she began to cry.

'I don't want to go back, I want to be with my mother!' she wept pitifully and then to me. *'I trusted you!'*

I felt a lump at the back of throat.

'I know, I'm sorry, I just didn't know what else to do.' I said lamely, and then as the paramedics came in and took over I returned to the bar as the resident whinger waggled his empty glass at me. But before he could so much as open his mouth I lifted a finger and waggled it back hissing, *'Don't you dare!'*

That particular incident is up there with a whole host of memorable experiences bordering on the dark side, like the time I witnessed my first bar brawl. Seeing it coming, watching it brewing, but unlike the situation with that poor girl in the lounge, I was in no position to stop it.

Picture the scene, if you will, it's a busy weekend night, the place is jamming and there's lots going on. Pool games, the television is on, the Juke box is blaring, and there are men, lots of men, throwing beer down their necks as they enjoy the end of the working week. The atmosphere is buzzing; the mood upbeat, and then I spot something. It isn't much, just a look, but it's enough, and for some inexplicable reason *I just know* trouble is coming.

I glance across to where the look was directed catch the eye of the one who is about to 'get it' and I couldn't be more surprised.

Interestingly he wasn't what I'd call one of my favourite customers- indeed he was less than savoury whose presence always filled me with unease. Yet on this occasion I saw fear in his eyes and almost felt sorry for him because Mr Menace, the pub bully had met more than his match and he knew it.

His would-be and soon-to-be assailant was also known to me, albeit vaguely, but enough to know he had a reputation for launching shockingly violent lightning attacks.

That they were both thugs was not in doubt, or the fact they were known to each other, and as I watched Mr Lightning smiling across the room at Mr Menace, it soon became obvious that the latter was afraid, very afraid. And so he needed to be. For not only was the other guy bigger than him, but he was also a lot meaner, and we both knew it!

It was a strange moment, looking into the eyes of a bully who's about to get his ass whooped by another bully. There was a storm coming and there was absolutely nothing he could do about it.

He nursed his pint nervously and waited hunched on his stool like a condemned man as I moved and flitted between pumps, the bulk of my boss and the other bar staff. I looked to see if they'd noticed what was about to kick off, but it was busy and noisy and they were obviously oblivious.

I felt helpless and my natural urge was to try and prevent this happening in some way. I looked to the bigger bully and he was smiling across again. I didn't even bother checking

out the response of his intended victim because there would
be that sickly look in his eyes and I cared enough to spare
his pride.

I pulled on the sleeve of my boss and he turned down to face
me, his face sheened in sweat.

'Yes, what is it!' he bawled jovially over the din.

I tugged some more to draw him down closer and said, 'I
think there's going to be a fight.'

'*What? What did you say?*'

Inwardly cursing his cauliflower ear that I'd had the
misfortune to end up with because I was stood on the wrong
side, I jerked my head round shouting, *'There's going to be
a fight!'* and nodded towards the two individuals before
drawing back and looking up at him expectantly.

His eyes lost their merry look as they swivelled between the
on-the-cusp attacker and his victim-to-be, and then it was as
though the shutters came down.

Without another word he merely straightened up and
commenced serving as though he hadn't heard a thing. I
stepped back in confusion. Something was about to kick off
in his pub and I may as well have said that the lager needed
changing.

I watched him for some moments as he resumed bantering
with the flock of young bucks at the bar before I realised
that he wasn't actually going to do anything, and so turning
my attention back to the room I immediately noticed that Mr
Lightning had disappeared.

I allowed myself to breathe a sigh of relief and picked up an
empty glass and resumed serving. As the jukebox boomed
and the crowd roared at some incident at the pool tables, I
flicked a glance at Mr Menace still sat haplessly at the bar
but he obviously wasn't buying it and quite right, too,
because suddenly the doors flew open behind him and in
charged his nemesis like some raging bull and began raining

punches down on him!

Those in the closest vicinity jumped back, beer sloshing, women shrieking, It was a shocking moment because it happened so fast, but the noise levels were such and the place so packed that everyone else continued on oblivious with their night.

True to form Mr Lightning had been crafty and had simply gone around so as to launch a surprise attack. Suffice to say, Mr Menace didn't stand a chance and disappeared from view quickly as his assailant beat him, literally, to the floor.

I heard a roar from behind me. It was my boss, and he was gesticulating wildly because the place was so jammed packed he couldn't get out of the hatch. It was an impressive display of *Landlord is outraged at fight in his pub but can't do anything about it* but of course there'll usually be a few regulars fuelled up nicely on Dutch courage who'll pile in and do the honours. And this is exactly what happened as they pulled the offending bully off his victim before hustling him to the door.

I didn't want to see anymore – much less what state Mr Menace was going to be in, but I did catch a glimpse of Mr Lightning before he was thrown into the night. He was still smiling as thought he'd merely exchanged pleasantries and was off home to his bed. It was a chilling moment and one that stayed with me.

Only two good things came out of that incident. Firstly, Mr Lightning Bully Number One was barred for life; and doubtless not wanting to revisit his humiliation, Mr Menace Bully Number Two barred himself and I never clapped eyes on either of them again.

In the early days I found many of the customers in this particular establishment fascinating, and although I never dared to voice them, I had trivial questions aplenty. Like, why did that man with the big nose always look so sad and talk to nobody but himself? Why was that customer always so rude when you went out of your way to be pleasant – and last but not least and this was a regular one! How did the girls who came in every weekend still look good by the end of the night when my carefully-applied make-up went into full clown status? How did they do it - and after several pints of strong lager, no less! I could never figure it out and I would gaze enviously at their pristine mascara as mine usually found its way down to my chin.

But as rough and ready as my introduction to bar work was, it was also very grounding and gave me great insight into people, personalities and when alcohol gets into the mix. There were never any airs or graces, anything but. You always knew exactly where you stood and if you could read your customers as the beer went down all the better!

Another interesting establishment was a well-known boozer, but for all the wrong reasons, and understandably I was a bit nervous during my first few shifts. As we all know most pubs have a bar and a lounge, and it is the latter that is usually the 'safe haven' unless you like a bit of spit and sawdust and the bar in this particular pub was no exception. If anything it was pretty notorious, and I was suitably awed when I first stepped behind the worn wooden counter and took in its inhabitants.

For the first time I had an understanding of what people meant when they talked about the 'Missing Link' - although there was enough here to have made a shipping chain! Jutting jaws, brutish heads, bristling brows, some even had no necks. I was agog. It was like walking into a different world – a prehistoric one – but they regarded me with bland disinterest and I was never more glad to be ignored.

There was no bar-side flirting here. No idle chatter or maudlin exchanges. I was just another barmaid; beer was the business here. Beer and the odd bust-up, and once I settled to this age-old agenda I found them all quite charming - in a rough-neck kind of way. They in turn, once I memorised their poison, progressed from one grunt to two and soon I preferred working the bar to the lounge.

This was due in part to the fact I'd become an avid people-watcher and found this tough and ready crew particularly interesting. It was like watching lions mixing it up with wolves, and for the most part there maintained an uneasy truce as this motley collection of Alpha males fraternised, ignored, or played cards with each other. But then something would happen. A wrong word. A look. And it would kick off, and when things kicked off, they really kicked off and chairs and bodies would fly!

I'd duck behind the bar as my boss would come running in yelling at me to get back to the lounge. *Was he kidding?* And miss all the fun! Forget all the bar-brawls you've seen in a Western – this was the real deal and it was exciting. I'd peep over the counter at the fist-flying melee but often as fast as it flared up it would quickly calm down, and as my boss would stomp back towards the lounge cursing loudly, he'd always spot me and just shake his head.

I wasn't there for long but long enough to see how it warranted its reputation. And although this pub has been renamed and refurbished many times over the years, the shadow of its heyday still hangs over it. I can never pass without a nostalgic inner tweak for those wild but heady days safe in the knowledge that the 'Missing Link' is still alive and kicking!

Another great character pub that has to go down as one of my favourites was for the fact there was *always* something going on. The customers were incredibly diverse, slightly tarnished around the edges but good fun as long as you kept on the right side of them. Whereas action in a pub would usually happen in the bar area, here the lounge wasn't fussy so it helped to stay alert at all times.

Take a gang of local hoodlums for instance; made up of tough-nuts and ex-jailbirds usually accompanied by a motley crew of womenfolk as flinty as their men! They would huddle conspiratorially in the furthest corner, heads bent, conversations intense, and the secrecy of their shenanigans would all but kill me with curiosity!

Occasionally, driven beyond suspense, I would sidle by on the pretext of collecting glasses and they'd cease talking until I'd passed. The only clue you'd have to their activities was when the police would drop in – which was frequently. But these guys were always one step ahead and made going AWOL a speciality. So when an officer would ask if you had seen so and so today, you'd shake your head and assume a vague look knowing damn well they were either hiding in the toilet or had just slipped out the back door.

A particular character of note was a local man called Sid. He was a long-whiskered one-eyed ex-sailor who blasphemed like a demon and could raise the roof with a scowl. He was only small but his presence was massively magnificent in a macabre kind of way, and when I first met him he practically frightened me to death!

His head would swivel and he'd fix you with one glaring eye, the seamed face taut and twisted as he'd growl and hiss, and on our first meeting I felt like poor *Nancy* caught up in the bar scene in 'Oliver' beset by some roistering drunk sent up from the depths of hell!

When in doubt about a customer I soon learned to look around and gauge the reaction of the other drinkers. Anyone dodgy, eyes would avert but stay watchful. If they were okay I'd be greeted with a sea of unconcerned faces. These became my pointers.

So when I first encountered the snarling specimen that was Sid, my eyes darted desperately around the room only to find everyone had gone quiet but was watching with what I can only describe as keen interest.

This threw me completely -what did it mean?

The question perplexed me and I finally got my answer when one of the regulars made a confession. They knew what Sid was like of course; they just wanted to see how I dealt with him. A baptism of fire cooked up for their own amusement but such stunts were typical. I knew I'd passed the test when I looked up from pulling a pint one day to find his one good eye twinkling at me.

Some people, however, were less fortunate, like the well-heeled individual who dropped in one day and ordered a pint in plummy tones. It was too much for Sid and he immediately unleashed the beast.

There are few things as funny as watching someone studiously trying to ignore the shenanigans of another, especially when they're right in your face. And as Sid the Imp cursed and capered we tried to keep a straight face as the poor man downed his pint in record time before making his escape!

My introduction to this age-old profession was at times brutal and bizarre, but it was never boring, and as I improved in my bar capabilities so did my confidence grow and I actually began to enjoy it.

There then followed on a succession of different bar jobs. All memorable for different reasons and all invaluable for showing me the ropes like how to make a pink gin.

This was in a posh ex-servicemen's club where I also developed a love for cryptic crosswords. This was due to a customer, who would buy a certain newspaper for that purpose, and we would lean, like two comrade-in-arms across the bar, heads lowered, brows furrowed as we parroted clues in feverish tones.

I particularly enjoyed working here because it was as safe as it was exclusive. It was membership only and an intercom system meant that anyone who was not invited could not come in. It was peaceful, civilised, a veritable sea of oasis - until I worked my first Rugby International.

Now international day is huge in Cardiff when the fans descend and all drinking establishments positively burst at the seams. So I was feeling suitably smug as I made my way up the stairs that morning expecting nothing more than a busier than usual day with the tele on.

How wrong was I!

'You're in the upstairs, bar, love.' My boss told me and there was something in his voice that made me do a double-take. There was a sheepish look in his eyes before they slid away from mine and I was immediately on my guard.

I had never been in the upstairs bar before; in fact I never knew one existed! The building was tall and large with unexplored doors and landings, so it was with no small trepidation that I made my way aloft and came into what one would describe more as a function room. A very *large* function room and my heart dropped like a stone.

The biggest TV projector screen I'd ever seen straddled an entire wall and the very sight of it sealed my doom. I'd drunk in enough pubs on match day to know that it gets busy. Crazy-busy. And I was supposed to serve the masses in here... *on my own?*

There was a tread on the stairs outside and the steward's son bounced in. He must've seen my stricken face because he clapped me on the back saying, 'Don't look so worried, Mandy, I'll be with you today!'

My spirits lifted considerably as we got on with setting up the bar and then I spotted the till, and this time my heart

truly did hit the floor. *What the...*
Now I can add up with the rest of them, and indeed had
become quite adept at totting up rounds. But there are times,
especially when it's busy, when a till that does it for you is
your best bar friend, and yet here before me was an old-
fashioned push-button effort that had probably fallen from
the ark before finding its way here like that board-game
from the film *Jumanji!*
I was horrified and touched an ancient button as you would
an unseen artefact as it dawned on me I would have to add
up *every* round for *every* customer amidst a cacophony of
sound you only really get to hear when there's a Rugby
International on, and I just knew it was all going to go
horribly wrong.
As it happened, it all went bearably ok – even when the
steward's son abandoned me for the second half. I ebbed
and flowed hour upon hour, sprinklers now off, calculations
for each round close enough as the ancient till and I simply
banged along together. As the crowd roared and the big
screen blared the tips came piling in.
'Take one for yourself, Mand.'
'Have a drink out of this, love.'
'Make sure you get a drink for yourself.'
Their generosity knew no bounds. The mood was high and
celebratory. Wales had won and I, for some reason, was
reaping the benefits as my tip-glass filled up and I realised
that I was actually doing a good job! The buzz was terrific.
It was also the day I learnt how to change a barrel and
handle a whole room full of large beery over-excited men.
The day passed into something of a blur with just a short
break for a sandwich before I was back on the pumps and
then finally, after a relentless eight hour shift, the room
began to empty and I was never more relieved when the
steward's son weaved into view.

'It's ok, Mand, you can get off now. I'll clear up.'
I didn't need telling twice! Exhausted didn't even cut it!
My brain was completely frazzled from a day of din and
adding up; arms aching and feeling like over-cooked strands
of spaghetti. My back hurt, my eyes stung, but all was paled
into significance by the deep ache in my feet.
I could almost hear them begging for mercy, for succour, for
sanctuary - anything! *Just get us off the bloody floor!*
They throbbed mercilessly but the end was in sight and I
ignored the agony all but running down the stairs so eager
was I to get out! What was more I was extremely hungry.
Starving in fact!
My veritable treasure trove of tips meant that I could have
whatever I wanted and sod the expense! Still on a high and
in desperate need of a treat, I made my way down the high
street like someone with all of the determination of a pilgrim
with the Holy Grail in sight! Instead of the usual take-out
burger, or a carton of curry and chips, I decided to really
push the boat out and 'eat posh'!
The place I had in mind was a well-known branded
restaurant that was renowned for large juicy steaks. I had it
in my mind and half-way to my belly; steak and chips
accompanied by a glass of wine or two. That was all I
wanted, and the image drew me on like a flaming torch, and
as I hobbled painfully in through the doors my empty
stomach gurgled loudly in anticipation.

The place was busy, it was International night after all and
every table taken, but hope beat eternal in my hungry heart
and my optimism was rewarded.
Tucked away in the furthest darkest corner, covered in a pile
of menu's and spare condiments was a lone table that would
seat no more than two; it was the perfect hideaway after
such a manic day and my stomach gurgled some more.

Now before I go any further, unaccompanied women popping into anywhere for a lone meal wasn't something you'd see very much in those days. This was in the early 80's when women were just starting to flex their shoulder pads in what was still a very Man's World. The fact there was a woman in 10 Downing Street meant absolutely nothing as I was about to discover.

As soon as the staff spotted me there was a rush.

To get me out.

'No, sorry, we're full.'

'I'm afraid we're fully booked.'

'Sorry, but we have no free tables.'

And I hadn't even opened my mouth!

I nodded to the perfect table in the perfect corner and said, 'What about that one? That would be alright.'

The waitress's were stumped for a moment before the tallest one with a haughty air I assumed was the supervisor piped up.

'Oh no, you can't sit *there!*'

I looked at her and then closely at the table.

Had I missed something?

'Why not?'

She shifted her feet uncertainly as her two counterparts waited respectively for her response. Tension was in the air with all of the pending drama of the O.K. Corral and I only wanted a steak.

'Well...it's in the corner, you'd be on your own...' she said lamely.

I regarded her steadily aware that my face had adopted a mulish look. My belly was by now in uproar at the cooking aromas and I wasn't going to give up without a fight.

'I've been on the go all day. I'm knackered. I'm absolutely starving and all I want to do is sit down and eat.'

It was a statement of fact, a declaration of intent, a desire so strong it would not be thwarted.

We stared at each other for some moments. She, looking impossibly groomed with not a hair out of place. Me, a sheen of sweat still on my face, my mascara speckled and smudged, and then suddenly it dawned on me...

The reason my request was being met with such resistance was because they thought I was on the game! They thought I was a prostitute coming in for substance after a day on the job! I nearly laughed out loud.

My rather inopportune and misleading statement of having been 'on the go all day' was obviously being taken literally. They assumed, judging not just by my crumpled appearance, because let's face it, a day behind a smoky bar awash with beer and testosterone is going to leave something of a mark, and they'd picked up on it – only in the *wrong* way!

My lips twitched. I was too tired to be outraged. The concept of being able to sit down and be waited upon had taken on such Herculean meaning I would've held my hand up to being Salome I so badly wanted that steak.

'Maybe you could sit over there?' suggested one of the waitress's and gestured vaguely into the restaurant proper. All I could see what a long table with lots of rowdy people sat around it sporting the odd balloon. 'We could pop a chair on the end there, I'm sure they wouldn't mind.'

'*Yes!*' said the supervisor with a kind of desperate hope. She was keen not to offend in case I *wasn't* a 'lady of the night', but equally she obviously though I was and this presented the perfect solution. 'Besides, it would be *much* better than being sat on your own.'

She looked at me, all but willing me to accept and I couldn't believe the effrontery that they would even consider foisting a complete stranger on what was obviously a private party.

'But I *want* to sit on my own. That's the whole point!'

We locked gazes.

'All I want to do is have something to eat and then I'll go...'
It was not an unreasonable request. Indeed it was more than
appropriate considering this was a restaurant, and even if I
had been a lady of the night; my coin was as good as anyone
else's. By now I was ready to commit murder and a mass one
at that if I didn't get my dinner and something transmitted.
With a curt nod she conceded and instructed one of the
waitresses' to clear and prepare the corner table with ill-
concealed grace. She could've thrown all of the menus up in
the air for all I cared. I'd won the battle, *I was going to eat!*
Service commenced as soon as I was seated, but in a stroppy
and resentful way that only further fuelled my amusement. I
will never forget this night, I thought, and I never have to
this day.

The way the plate was banged down. My glass of wine
slopped. But none of it mattered. I enjoyed my meal
immensely and refused to be belittled – even when they
presented me with the bill as soon as I'd taken my last chip.
Their behaviour was unpleasant to the point of insulting, and
as I fished amongst my tips for the right money I vowed
there and then that if I ever had cause to serve a woman
dining on her own, I'd ensure a courteous welcome. Suffice
to say I never darkened the door of that particular eatery
again.

As my skills grew it soon became apparent to me that I
actually enjoyed working a bar and meeting all kinds of
people. But equally was the knowledge I wasn't really cut
out to be anything grander than a barmaid in a backstreet
pub.
This was made clear to me during my first stint in an
upmarket establishment. The fact I had to wear a dickey bow
didn't help. Neither did the requisite skirt and fishnet tights.
But the money was good and the place was snazzy and the

team I worked with made it worth the while.

We were a close bunch. Working a large chic establishment back in the day when Yuppies ruled and Beaujolais was all the rage. Our *clientele* were the cream of local business and we were expected to scrape and grovel accordingly.

This particular job spec however, didn't go down well with the majority of us because we were young, vivacious people and soon these personalities began to show through.

'You're being too familiar,' was one admonishment. *'Don't be so friendly,'* was another.

For some reason the management wanted to run a superficial ship, whereby 'we' the lowly staff were expected to show suitable deference to 'them' who were our customers and at all times 'know our place.'

Ironically, the well-heeled customers who patronised the business actually enjoyed the lack of formality and we were a popular crew.

My particular speciality was to impersonate the character Angie Watts from Eastenders. I'd greet and banter in loud cockney tones and the punters loved it. The bosses, however, did not. And so hostilities began in earnest.

It was around this time the 10ft Amazonian Woman first began to emerge and she couldn't have timed it better. In a bid to rein us in we were informed that any drinks bought by the customers were no longer to be taken by the staff. Our jaws dropped open at that, and word soon spread to the *clientele.* They vigorously objected to such blatant unfairness and insisted we be allowed our perk. The management conceded with much baring of the teeth, and secretly we sniggered but they weren't finished with us yet!

The next bombshell was that the cost of the uniform – originally advertised as being provided free of charge – would be forthwith deducted from our wages. We were aghast! We hadn't seen this one coming and it shook us to the core because we couldn't do anything about it, indeed, what could you do when the management held the very purse strings that fed, never mind clothed you!

We murmured and muttered amongst ourselves and there began a simmering of rebellion amongst the ranks that erupted at their next move, and this time *we* meant business when we learned they were going to commandeer our tips! It was a bitter blow and we were suitably outraged. Our tips were excellent, and usually ensured a good pay-out at the end of the month. With barely suppressed fury we handed our keys over as the cash box *we* had purchased out of *our* tips sat on the desk beneath the self-satisfied smile of the GM.

It was simply too much to bear and that night after work we all gathered in a basement bar nearby for a Council of War. We were of the belief that because the business was not doing as well as it should, by dipping into our hard-earned tips the management had hoped to fill in the gaps and that we would lose a large percentage – big time!

There was only one thing that we could do but we had to be in it together. Feelings were running so high at this point, no doubt helped on by a few pints of snakebite, even the chef who was usually the bosses man agreed that action had to be taken.

I remembered the barmaids from my first bar job and how uncompromising they'd been, and drawing on this I put forward the argument that nothing but a tough stance would do.

The next morning we made up a posse from each department made their way to the office with all the dignity of a die-hard rabble, and the bosses' faces were a veritable picture as we strode in.

I had been selected as the spokesperson and empowered by

my newly-found status, felt myself rise a few inches as I
presented our complaint - the Amazonian Woman had
woken...

By taking our tips, in addition to uniform deductions that
had not been pre-agreed, meant we were going to suffer
financially. Besides, the cost of the uniform wasn't in the
original job spec – indeed it had been advertised a *free and
provided!* What were they thinking! It wasn't fair and quite
simply we weren't going to put up with it and what was
more we wanted our tip-box back!

The bosses were visibly shaken. They hadn't expected this
or the boldness of our approach. But we had no other card to
play other than threatening strike action unless they
overturned their decisions.

They did, with alacrity, and handed the tip box back right
there on the spot.

I felt myself rise a bit more as they eyed me with renewed
respect. There was also angry resentment there, of course,
barely suppressed but it was there. But something inside me
had changed and I wasn't frightened of them anymore.

Feeling 10ft tall I led the way back to the main serving area
to share the good news with the others where they waited
anxiously.

We had done it. We had won. We were cock-a-hoop and it
was difficult, admittedly, walking around the next couple of
weeks trying not to smirk as we savoured our victory.

But some wars are simply not to be won and in a devastating
turn-about-face the management metaphorically tore up our
agreement and threw it back in our face. They would be
taking back control of the tips and the decision was final!

We were stunned, but not broken, and one by one sallied
forth until all they had left was the chef and one waitress.

Work was in abundance in those days; you could go from
one position to the next quite easily, but we had reckoned

without their clout!
Well-connected locally their response was to put the word
out and suddenly we found ourselves blacklisted and turned
away from every job! This was my first encounter with the
power of the 'Old Boys' Network' and not something to be
underestimated. But they reckoned without the clout of our
old clientele who were suitably appalled at our treatment.
So with open warfare within the aforementioned network,
our old customers ensured that doors *would* be opened where
before they'd been closed, and we all parted ways with no
sense of regret as the business fell flat on its face.
There is a moral in the story here, I guess, about pushing
buttons and abusing one's position because bullying doesn't
pay – and it certainly didn't in this situation. There's also
the matter of moving with the times. Accepting that old-style
service doesn't cut it when the *clientele* wants new - and the
customer is always right, right?
I often wonder how differently things could've worked out if
the management had just bent with the breeze and allowed
their staff that bit of leeway to be themselves, which brings
me neatly onto the next place that wanted the complete
opposite!

In this particular establishment you were encouraged to
actively engage, encourage and all but titillate the senses of
each customer with a combination of frolics and friendliness
more suited to an old-style saloon. It was an American-
themed set-up, relatively new and a nightmare. The innate
falsity of it all grated on me - tremendously. We were, for
the most part, Welsh, not thigh-slapping Americans and as
friendly as the natives of Cardiff are, we have our limits.
Admittedly in its day it was a funky hang-out. One of the
best, the most hip to be seen but I hated it.
Again I had to don that accursed dickey bow with a swanky

waistcoat - but at least they allowed trousers and of course there was the requisite name badge. Why I had to have my name pinned on my chest was beyond me. This was quite a new concept at the time and I wasn't alone in my dislike of it.

But then this was no ordinary bar, it was a *cocktail bar* whereby you had to learn the ingredients of over twenty cocktails off by heart before they'd even consider you for an interview.
'Come and work with me,' he said, 'it'll be fun!' he said. Famous last words of an ex work-colleague who was thriving in this new-fangled environment. The fact he'd been promoted to Head Waiter in under a month meant he was already enslaved but to my mind for all the wrong reasons. I felt an inner resistance and it wasn't just towards the dickey bow. I had no interest in the complexities of mixing one spirit with another and adorning them with pink brollies. Cocktails were an alien concept to a girl who drank pints of cider, and the thought of having to learn how to make up two dozen of the buggers was for me, a calling practically beyond the pale. But I allowed myself to be persuaded and duly got my head stuck into the world of *crème de menthes* and *Curacao* with a feeling of being back in the school chemistry lab. After a week of hard study I cracked it but my heart wasn't in it.
I have to say that of all the interviews I've ever done, and there have been many, this had to be the most odd. I couldn't believe that success depended on how much gin you put into a Singapore sling, or what garnishes constituted the perfect 'Pink Lady'. It felt almost surreal as I babbled about 'Bloodhounds' and strove to recall what liquor to use in an 'Aviation'. Suffice to say it was a torturous process but I passed. Barely!

It's my belief that when you're not interested in something, even if you force-feed information repeatedly into your brain, there's an open crack somewhere and all of that

knowledge simply seeps away until there are just a few cherries rolling around. And so it was with this job and their pesky drinks and within days I was struggling.
I shook when I was supposed to stir; stirred when I should have shaken. I'd have to hiss for instruction as my mind went a blank and I longed for the simplicity of hand pumps and optics. Because it was a fast-moving environment you were expected to serve, swish, swoop and sparkle effortlessly as punters bawled their orders over the music that couldn't have been louder if you'd been at a rock concert. Yet you were still expected to introduce yourself with each new customer as if the name badge wasn't enough, and smile with enforced jollity because, hey, this is the place to be and look, my name is Mandy!
Oh the hell of it... and if that wasn't bad enough cue the lack of lip-reading skills. This is something I believe you acquire over time and so I often got orders wrong; *Very* wrong!
And then there were the flakes. Those of the chocolate variety, boxes and boxes of them sat like *manna* from heaven in the fridges. As a bona-fide and committed chocoholic, such temptation was practically beyond a saint, and I became adept at stuffing them into my mouth at every given opportunity.
Such proclivity was frowned upon; the odd flake, yes, but I couldn't help myself. They became the ultimate comfort food as my cocktail skills became increasingly calamitous. It was unfortunate for me at this time a new manager had started who was keen to strut his stuff and I knew my days were numbered.
He was a tiny little fellow with a big mouth and an attitude to match. He'd stride about the place like a mini-Hitler barking orders and - horror of horrors - was also obsessive about stock control! Yet still I found myself reaching into the fridge like an afflicted Eve intent upon the apple, and still the flakes went down.
The day of reckoning finally came and I felt myself stiffen as he poked about behind the bar before coming to the fridges that he regarded with a critical eye.
'These flakes are looking a bit low,' he said and I fleetingly

hoped I'd wiped my mouth properly after the last intake.
'Oh?'
It was a pathetic attempt at innocence and we both knew it,
because turning to face me he snapped, 'In fact we're on the
third box in a week! Care to tell me how?'
It wasn't a question, more of a demand as he assumed full
Hitler-persona. His voice was hard, his eyes like gimlets and
I gazed back haplessly. For once I was speechless. What
could I say? Yes, I'm really sorry but I've got this flake
fetish, you see...
I lifted my shoulders and gave what I thought was a wide-
eyed Bambi look but he wasn't having any of it.
'Well?'
His bark was so nasty I wasn't going to give him a chance to
bite, and as all pretence dropped away we eyed each other
with open hostility. I knew I was busted and he wanted me
out. Besides my incessant lack of chocolate control there had
also obviously been complaints. My 'concoctions' were on a
par with Frankenstein's laboratory no one needed to tell me
that. Their faces when they took the first sip told me all I
needed to know, especially when I'd see them slip off to
lodge an official complaint and I had been getting it in the
ear daily. Flake-Gate was simply the cherry on the cake and
he didn't hold back.
I endured his tirade indifferently until he came out with a
remark that not even I could ignore.
'...and besides, you're obviously more suited to a back-street
pub where the barmaids are usually fat lazy slobs anyway!'
Fat!??? I was a size 10 and as skinny as a whippet!
I held up a hand that itched to dispense a slap but I
restrained myself. I'd take the rap for being cocktail-
incompetent, I'd even take it on the nose for not keeping it
out of the fridge, but I would not be called lazy or fat and
launched a vigorous counter-attack ably assisted by my
Amazonian Lady. There then followed on an unseemly
exchange of words that saw me finally stomp off to my
locker with the parting shot of a moist dark place where he
could stick his dickey bow and chocolate flakes!
With the staff agog I made a flourishing exit and it wasn't

going to be the first job I would stomp out of. Around this
time I discovered I was actually a bit of a 'stomper'. In fact,
if I am to be brutally honest, I am a serial and serious
stomper and once I've stomped I rarely stomp back. I think
this may have had something to do with my emerging
Amazonian alter-ego, still in its baby-stages admittedly, but
then giants do have a tendency to stomp so I'm guessing this
just kind of came with the territory.

As I mentioned earlier, work wasn't hard to find in those
days but it was the last time I would work a bar that didn't
have *real drinks* and where appearance was more important
than personality. You could keep your James Bond bar
tenders with their long-sufferings smiles and fancy manners-
it was back street boozers and slobbiness ALL the way!

Personality and a certain level of competence is all you need
to be a good bar tender. I really do believe that. You can be
the most handsome man, the most gorgeous girl, but if can't
pour a decent pint or are poker-faced with a sense of humour
by-pass, then forget it. There are few things worse than
someone who casts a shadow when you're out to enjoy
yourself. And besides, there's always the risk of becoming
prime bait as there's nothing some punters like more than
taking people down from their high horse.

The ability to master some basic adding up is also a huge
help. Tills weren't always mechanical in some of the places
I worked, and as someone who struggled mightily with
maths at school; the discovery that I was adept at ale-house
arithmetic was as surprising to me as it was to mankind
beholding the first eclipse!

By the time I'd worked a few places and got into the swing,
I found not only did I love bar work, but that I actually
became very good at it and could handle three rounds
simultaneously and retain each count in my head.

Changing barrels, however, was a task I never really enjoyed
as you heaved and straddled great weights about. Fortunately
there were usually customers at hand who were willing to
roll up their sleeves and get all Sir Galahad for a free pint.
There was also another reason for this; beer barrels are

usually kept in cellars and cellars are, how shall we say, not always the kind of place you want to be in on your own – but more about that later...

But ultimately, and I can't stress it enough, the key part of being a good bar person is that you've got to like people. Lots of them! All kinds of them! And treat each and every one as though they are the only person between you and that pump on the plant. For the most part customers love attention and expect to be pandered to. Whether they're the slobbering drunk or a strait-laced snoot – anyone who's willing to part with their money is entitled to good service and, if you can manage it, a smile. Even if the latter fails to appreciate the gesture, most people like to feel that their business *matters*.

I learnt that early on because punters spot everything and woe betide you if you show favouritism and always, always, serve the person who is next. Some people are very good at projecting themselves at a busy bar as they all but thrust a glass in your face, a maniacal gleam in their eye that demands *you'd better serve me! Next!*

It's a robust form of bullying and being a female in a predominantly male environment, this had a tendency to come with the turf. Not that the fairer sex were above using the same tactics and sometimes they could also be even scarier. (Being called a 'baggage', for instance, is particularly memorable when I refused an old lady her rum after time, as was the litany of curses she rained down on my head that would not have been out of place in a scene from Macbeth!)

And so there you are, suddenly the most wanted, the most needed, the most desirable person in the world because your hands are key to the pump, the beer and the till. It's really busy, the punters are three-deep at the bar and they all want serving NOW! This was when I used to employ what I called the 'slidey eye'. I would sweep the bobbing heads mentally putting in order who's next rather than the one who is shouting the loudest.

Ah, yes, it's that hopeless-looking fellow all but squeezed into the corner, his flailing empty glass held aloft with no real expectation of being replenished. So aggressive are his neighbours they all but squash him into oblivion but you've got him in your sights and there's no room for argument - he is next. Ignoring the growls of outrage you glide serenely across and take his glass and are rewarded by a smile of such gratitude it makes your heart glow. Even the howls of protest fall onto deaf and indifferent ears because the hopeless-looking one was *next* and that's an end to it. Muttered insults are equally ignored as you continue to slide your eyes continually until they alight on the next customer, and so it went on.

Being the recipient of a customer's frustration is all part of the course and donning a thick skin is nearly as important as releasing the Amazonian when needed. There were, and will always be, those who will take umbrage, look down on you, speak out of turn for no other reason that they can. Working in the service industry means you're open to all manner of abuse - it is an essential and unavoidable part of the beast. Developing a good sense of humour and a no-nonsense approach when things go too far, was, I found the best tools at my disposal when faced with a hostile reception. But even more importantly was knowing when to employ which one. Take the 'Rum Lady' for instance. A regular tippler of a certain age who always looked as though she put her make-up on in the dark. She obviously had a drink problem and could turn on the spin of a coin. This I discovered when I refused her a drink after Time and was liberally treated to all manner of insults, the most memorable being called 'a baggage'.
Now bear in mind that I was only nineteen at the time and was suitably bemused at being labelled with a name that went out with the Ark. But I knew better than to giggle for there were knives in her stare so I restrained my mirth and accepted the insult mutely.
Then there was the time I had a stand-off with a customer who had clearly had enough but wasn't prepared to accept the decision quietly. Despite a barrage of insults as to my sexual proclivity and possible alternative employment, I

bore the abuse stoically until this lovely individual finally staggered outside with high dudgeon in his heart.

I watched in disbelief as he began lighting matches and throwing them down the cellar grating and on to the mats below. *He was trying to set the place on fire!*

He nearly succeeded too, as smoke began to billow out and seeing this I ran through the pub shouting *'Fire! Fire!'*

This valiant attempt to save my fellow-man fell on deaf ears as one or two looked up with mild interest before returning to their pints. It was half past ten on a Saturday night and there was *no way* anyone was going to evacuate whilst there was still forty minutes drinking time on the clock!

The landlord, however, did take me seriously and ran down to the cellar with an extinguisher and a few choice words before putting the fire out. The complete lack of concern from the customers that night reverberates with me still as I recall my panic believing the gas bottles would ignite and blow us all to space!

But then this was the pub of Sid the Seaman and Cardiff's equivalent to the Krays so in all fairness I shouldn't have been too surprised.

More dangerous yet, I found, were the customers who insisted they buy you a drink before assuming ownership of your person for the remainder of the night. I could never quite figure this one out – how was a glass of lager supposed to ensure your undivided attention? And why was there always nastiness when you made it quite clear it would take more than half a pint!

Such encounters were as rare as they were unexpected, but they did happen and doubtless they still do. There must be some kind of time warp going on with these people - the deluded belief that they're back in medieval times when barmaids were wenches and up for a penny and a roll in the hay.

I developed a nose for them, a kind of sixth sense. Dealing with their affront upon refusing a cider was ultimately more appealing than the outraged beast afterwards when you rebuffed their grappling paws.

That is the uglier and seldom seen side of a life in service;

sexual predation and unpredictable punters with a penchant for a penny-lay. On the positive side, however, good-natured banter and genuine friendships have been forged when all has been required is your company and a good head on their pint. That is a healthy relationship. Fostered to a level that is comfortable for both bar person and customer where laughter sustains you and banter is to be enjoyed.

One of the best places I ever worked in was a small social club that was a two-tier affair and a hot-house of diversity. On the first floor you had the main bar, and above a lounge area where folk-nights were hosted. Here you would have the pleasure of listening to all manner of musicians and singers as they shared their talents for worthy causes like the Miners' Strike and displaced Iraqi's.
Downstairs you could join the *craic* and be a part of the babble, but upstairs was a different matter. Musicians here took the business of entertainment very seriously and upon entrance you had to all but take a vow of silence when someone was in full song. All well and good, but this could make slightly awkward when trying to lip-read and mumble at the same time! I lost count of the times I would be frowned at or reprimanded from the mic for having spoken above a whisper or laughed too loudly.
Fortunately I was never offended and found it funny that you were expected to sit still like schoolchildren. My response was to put a finger to my lips by way of apology whilst ignoring the devilment of the other wanting to join it with a gesture of its own!
It was such a fun place to work and with very nice bosses who made it an added joy. I also made a lot of friends, the acoustic players particularly, who regularly forgave my natural high spirits as a matter of course.
Musicians and pubs go together and coming from a musical family myself, working the upstairs shift was always a pleasure. And despite not being able to read a note I enjoyed warbling along nevertheless when the occasion demanded it.

Another great place was a village pub in the heart of North

Wales – Snowdonia National Park, in fact. The village might have been small, but the personalities of its people were not. It was unique for the fact you had such a mix, yet rarely was there any trouble. After years of having worked rough-end bars where you had to be careful where you looked and what you said, it was refreshing to be able to relax completely and enjoy the banter without being taken the wrong way. I have very fond memories of being sat out on the veranda beneath summer wisteria, or *cwtched* up by a roaring log fire during the cold months.

A particular memorable night one winter was when some drunken golfers thought they'd entertain us with an impromptu strip. They were noisy and obnoxious and probably had wives at home who would've been horrified at their exploits. At first it was amusing until they progressed to waggling their bits in your face. Not even my quip 'That looks like a willy only smaller' had any effect and off they went for a streak down the village. My boss, who remains a good friend to this day, thought she'd teach them a lesson and locked them out in the snow.

As they beat down the door begging to be let back in, all of a sudden being stark bollock naked wasn't so much fun after all and they duly crept up to their beds shivering and shrunken. We still have a good giggle about it to this day! There were stop-ons and parties, more stop-ons and a few more parties, and I spent several happy years here being paid to serve, laugh and make merry! But there comes a time when something happens and the laughter stops, when the eye that once glittered becomes jaded, when being of service has become a chore and something inside you snaps. But more about this later...

HOUSEMAID OR HOTEL SLAVE

If you've never done housekeeping for a job, then believe me, you should try it! Life is not complete until you've tasted the delights of toilet-scrubbing and finding turds in the bed! How house maids throughout the centuries must have suffered with this one I can easily fathom, because cleaning up other peoples' shite is certainly not for the fainthearted!

I began my 'apprenticeship' in a very large dwelling that had just over two dozen bedrooms of varying sizes and a huge downstairs area. Three storeys, lots of stairs, and one woman; I was that woman. A young woman just into my early twenties, granted, but the workload was so punishing you'd have thought me more of a pensionable age by the time I hobbled out. To say that I was exhausted was an understatement!

This large old-fashioned establishment was run by a formidable foreign couple. She was thin, ramrod straight and had a way of barking at you rather than speaking. He in contrast was large, fleshy and had an amiable air that was very misleading for the speed with which he could change when he didn't get his way.

I was in awe of them both and how they managed because

they were well into their sixties. But they were like a well-oiled machine and under their no-nonsense tutelage I soon became a well-oiled cog.

I'd start at eight, just in time to start clearing down the breakfast tables and would wash and then dry every last spoon and plate before being offered a left-over sausage that I would gobble down gratefully. Working in a kitchen that still retains a plethora of extreme cooking smells is akin to torture if you're hungry, and as a 'breakfast-skipper' I was no exception.

Then I would have to relay the tables and clean the dining room before moving on to the hallways and lounge. Next came the stairs and then the rooms where waited the next torture; beds with blankets. Sheets and blankets - blankets and sheets. Aaaarrrgghh!! I don't think Mrs 'Mussolini' as I secretly had nicknamed her had ever heard of duvets, but as an ex-nurse she knew everything there was to know about hospital corners and God help me if I didn't get them right! There is a world of difference, I know, between symmetrical folding and just stuffing the loose bits in, but stuffing can be done neatly and besides, who's going to notice once the bedspread is on? And for that matter, who would even care! Mrs Mussolini, obviously. Sometimes she would go behind me checking my work like a silent sheet-assassin looking for an untucked corner. Upon hearing that bark I'd roll my eyes and trot back to where she'd be stood bristling, bed spread held aloft and my 'hospital corner' looking more 'field hospital.'

She'd tut and shake her head before showing me *once again* how to do it and made it look so easy I could cry! And no, I never got the hang of it. Ever! Another item on the list of 'nowt can do' alongside my cocktail skills and inability to throw the javelin.

But whilst she was hard she wasn't hard-hearted, and there

were random acts of kindness. Indeed I was to call on them many years later for some help that they were only too happy provide with some runaway guests.

The workload, however, was punishing and I left after a few months to somewhere where they had 'proper bedding' (duvets) and more staff.

Being a cleaner, of any description is very hard work. It can be dirty, back-breaking, bemusing and at times shocking, but it's also very rewarding and a great way to keep in shape. Of all the jobs in service this one is probably looked down upon the most – with the exception of the kitchen porter who is just one step below. You either become invisible when you don the mop, or else someone whom it's okay to all but click the finger at. Rare is the boss who sees a diamond instead of a scrub-rock. Precious are your services to those who appreciate all the graft you put in so that they can sleep between crisp sheets and tinkle merrily down a sparkling loo!

I've done many cleaning jobs in my time, including pot-washing, but the two most memorable was scrubbing toilets in an office block and being head of a team in a busy country house.

In desperate need of money I braced myself for bog-duty when a friend of a friend of a friend put the job forward. It was only temporary but it was good honest work. Thankfully it was also after office hours so you could slink in through the main doors in the hope no one would see you that would perhaps know a friend of a friend of a different friend - because there's something infinitely 'dirty' about cleaning toilets.

Indeed if I could've got away with putting a bag over my head I'd have done so and happily, or else snap a mask over my face like the Secret Sh*thouse Scrubber. But then I was

still in my twenties and had a long way to go before I'd be
like one of those crones who'd sally forth in a pink bib-coat
bearing a mop with all the pride of a musketeer before
vigorously scrubbing the floor for the fortieth time that day.
I can recall the awe in which I beheld these underground loo
attendants when I was a small child; the tightly-curled hair,
the gimlet eye, the outraged squawk if you so much as tried
to dribble without paying your penny.
These guardians of such ghastly but much-needed places had
pride in their position; a sense of self amidst the constant
flow of the weak-bladdered population. A nose that was
impervious to the stench of urine - and for that they were
formidable and admirable for their dedication to a job few
could do!
Me? I sloped from cubicle to cubicle, holding my breath in-
between and dreading what I'd find when I got there; wipe,
wipe, scrub, scrub, flush, flush and then get the hell out of
Dodge!
My workmates were an interesting lot. A raggle-taggle of all
types and ages with a penchant for soap operas and a strict
pecking order. As the newest addition, naturally I was the
last in line, and if I was lucky I might gain, albeit fleetingly,
the airy attentions of those higher up the ladder. Being the
main duster or the one who handled the hoover was
obviously a role of dizzying heights and it bemused me that
they should be so condescending when we were all, at the
end of the day, a bunch of scrubbers. Sometimes I look back
on that brief spell of life with a kind of detached fascination
and wonder and think was that really me wielding a toilet
brush and pushing a trolley round like some Bog-Lady of the
Night? It doesn't bear thinking about; the sights I had to
face, the smells I stoically endured; but I'll spare you all that
because some things are best left behind and firmly down the
pan!

A more 'genteel' and yet no less pongy job at times is the role of chambermaid – a scrubber with a definite step up the ladder! And oh, how the hotels and motels, the inns and outhouses masquerading as accommodation wouldn't function without them! The housekeepers, the cleaners, call them what you like; they are the semi-hidden heroines and hero's who make this world a nicer and much sparklier place to live.

Having worked in various establishments over the years and dealt with more beds than a bedbug, I was truly, if I am to be honest, swept away by a beautifully appointed and very old country hotel up in the hills of North Wales.
Olde-worlde and steeped in history, I was immediately seduced and accepted the position of Head Housekeeper with alacrity – although in hindsight, Chief Slave would have been more appropriate, and it was this position that left me with a life-long hatred of doing laundry ever and using an iron.
What could've caused such domestic trauma, I hear you cry! Come with me and I'll show you my day – and this was a typical day in the land of hotel housekeeping with the added torment of an in-house laundry that had broken the spirit of those made of stronger stuff than I. It gave a small insight into how life must have been for the humble housemaid when Victoria sat on the throne and labour was at the mercy of the masters. If you think all that went out with the bustles and the bonnets then think again! Old-style expectations are still up and running, the only difference is that you don't have to curtsey or wear a mob cap!
It's 7am, you arrive bleary-eyed and muster a quick sort of the laundry and what needs doing. As the washers and the

driers begin to tumble and roll, you then proceed to the cleaning cupboard and take up your tools for the day. Make your way then to the furthest point, which is the lounge and begin working backwards through all the communal areas including the bar, foyer and toilets.

Ignore the reception staff that have now arrived and are sat cosily in the office sipping coffee. Keep your eyes on the job in hand and repress all feelings of envy and resentment.

Go back to the laundry room and tangle yourself up for a couple of hours as you manhandle queen-size sheets and get the roller press going. Smile as you fold and press, turn and fold; empty washing machine contents into dryers, entangle with more sheets.

Breakfast is now over so prepare to receive the mountain of napkins that is thrown in for your attention. Duly sling into the machine and keep pressing the endless piles of pillowcases whilst trying not to lose the will to live.

Towels need attending; they are finally dry. Hand towels there, please, shower mats there. Yes, you'll need to start another pile for the bath sheets and don't forget the bath robes. Fold and keep folding, yes, yes, keep going, there are loads more to do yet and we haven't even hit the bedrooms!

Two hours later the mountains of linen sit waiting as the Restaurant manager bustles back for the napkins. Chef has also been in during this time and slung down his whites. Duly you wash them and dry them then start to press in readiness for tonight's service. Of all the laundry in that god-forsaken room, Chefs' white are the worst! Never, in all your years have you wielded an iron to no avail, but press on, literally, you do because better the whole place go up in flames and your wrist fall off than Chef find the slightest crease in his whites!

You grit your teeth and wrangle that iron with such hatred in your heart it screams all-out rebellion. But you soldier on until the creases are barely perceptible and then flex the aching muscles of your poor forearms you will at this point seriously question your place in the Universe.

Right, time to go upstairs but first we need the list and the keys. Off we toddle to the main office where the reception staff are now on their second coffee accompanied by a croissant or two. This time their little oasis of calm is a little harder to ignore as they frown and regard you with thinly veiled contempt. We are the underdogs, we know, and they make it their business that we never forget it.

Grabbing at the keys and upon being presented the list we hastily repair to the upper confines of the house and start stripping.

Stripping, the bane of every housekeeper because it's much less work if the guests are staying over; an ideal morning is with as little strips as possible but on occasion, I'm afraid, every guest will be checking out.

It is the unspoken rule that no trip downstairs is ever wasted, and so you load yourself up with as much laundry as you can carry before staggering back up with all the clean that goes into the linen cupboard.

It is relentless, because as you strip your way through the rambling house you are back and fore, back and fore constantly, either to the aforementioned cupboard or back down to the hell-hole.

By mid-morning we're allowed to take a ten minute break. It's lovely outside so let's climb through the fire escape window and sit on the grass over there. It's okay because we're on the blind side of the hotel so no one can see us. We lower ourselves down with a groan and breathe deeply of the good clean air that doesn't smell of acrid cleaning chemicals and more dubious bedroom aromas.

Time for a smoke perhaps, something to eat and drink, glad

to see you've brought a banana. It's important you learn the best fast foods to keep your strength up because we're not even halfway through the day yet.

Break over, we clamber inside and it's back to the slog. Rooms, laundry, laundry, rooms; you're up and down more times than a Masai Warrior, and by lunchtime you're seriously starting to flag.

The rooms are large, the bathrooms roomier, and each has a shower *and* a bath with tiles galore, and trust me, over time you will develop a hatred for these porcelain squares.

Of all the housekeeping duties bathrooms are by far the worst, and the requisite rubber gloves a debatable godsend as your hands slowly cook to mush within them as inwardly you ask the same question again and again; *why do people have to pee on the seat! How on earth can you leave* that *floating about when you must* know *that the housekeeping will find it? And what the f**k is THAT!*

A cacophony of endless enquiries keeps you company as you deal with all manner of personal *faux pas* until sometimes it's too much to resist and you've just got to *know!* Slinking into the office on some pretext or another you'll find yourself casually asking who stayed in room 5 last night, because you have to have a name just to convince yourself that the guests in question had actually been human.

And then there are the beds. Queen-sized and faffy but easily done when there's two of you; it's when you're on your own that the leg-work begins in earnest as you scuttle between sides at least half a dozen times cursing volubly. But when the bedspread's on and it all looks really pucker its then on to the polishing and primping and refilling the hospitality tray.

On occasion you'll find yourself eyeing the packets of chop chip, and sometimes a packet will seemingly self-combust causing the odd cookie to catapult its way into your mouth without even a crumb left to indicate that this had occurred. But I wouldn't worry too much about it if I were you; such perils come with the job.

Of course, I hasten to add that although the odd bit of biscuit may find its way into an empty belly, trust is paramount when dealing with peoples' possessions, and if, on the rare occasion a tip was left in the room, you hand it in immediately. Never try to get cute and palm it for yourself, like one cleaner who was spectacularly caught out when the boss did a spot-check because he had planted it!

There could be no excuses and off he was marched from the premises and quite right, too; if you're willing to put your job on the line for a fiver then what else would you be capable of?

Mind you, it always amazed me the kind of things that guests would leave out in their room; wallets, jewellery, credit cards, cash, their faith in their fellow-human beings and the staff was phenomenal. But what probably amazed me more than anything else were those who came to stay and brought with them their *nu-nu's* - yes, you read that right; *nu-nu's!*

Usually found in the domain of children of a certain age, but certainly not exclusively. Some habits are just too hard to break, I guess, and so it was not unexpected to find all manner of things sat on beds and or draped across pillows, and it was always with a bemused sense of respect that I would put teddy back like-so, or take care not to bin a rag that looked like one of our cleaning cloths, or, and the most memorable of all, rearrange a whole host of *nu-nu's* that all but took over the bed!

This sticks in my mind because it was so unbelievably quirky and excessive, for there were no fewer than six of them, all doll-sized and sat, propped up against the pillows

waiting for me at turn-down!
Now I wasn't raised with an excess of dolls and cuddly toys,
and so coming upon this motley collection came as
something of a shock. Their appearance stopped me in my
tracks, a disconcerting medley of glass eyes staring, with the
exception of the homepride man – yes, there was even a
doll-sized figure of him!
It was bizarre, but as we offered a turn-down service and as
these *nu-nu* were obviously much-loved travelling
companions I duly tucked them all in before popping the
foil-covered mints on the paws of teddy.
Let it not be said I never showed anything less than
exemplary respect for a person's *nu-nu*'!

But forgive me; I move ahead of myself, the whole subject
of the turn-down comes later. For here we still are, stripping,
making, cleaning, hoovering, humping sacks of laundry up
and down the stairs in between wrestling bouts with the
washing, but we've broken the back of the main house and
it's time now for another break.
Cue your 30 minutes for lunch and weather permitting, its
back outside onto the grass. This is a more relaxed affair but
potentially lethal, it's hard to get going afterwards and
you've the stable block to do yet and yet even more laundry
in that hole from hell but let's not think about that right
now.
That half hour seems to fly by and you feel slightly
replenished, but there is an intense and communal reluctance
to return to the slog, yet you heave yourself up and set to it
anyway.
Impromptu chatter sustains you as you lug all of the cleaning
equipment across to the outside accommodation and then
return with armloads of linen. We're on the home-run now
but you know you're going to have at least another half hour

added in that damned laundry before you can get out, home, and finally collapse.

It's 3 o'clock and the last room is nearly done; all you need is one of the camp beds that is stored in the attic over in the main part of the house but no one wants to get it – and certainly on their own.

The room through which the attics are accessed is at the very top of the house in what was once the servant's quarters and that particular part of the building has what one would call, 'an atmosphere'.

There are no volunteers and maybe it's best if I don't send you or you might never come back, like the one lady who lasted only one shift – but then it is a very old building and so what do you expect? But more about that later...

As Head Housekeeper it's left to me to step up to the plate, and so I make my way up the narrow dark stairs and feel my skin prickling as I keep my eyes forward and hum a random tune. Word has it that someone did away with themselves up in this part of the house, but you try not to think about it or fall down the stairs in your haste to get out.

Soon we have the extra bed laid up and it is with huge and happy relief that we turn the final key in the final lock before returning to reception. There are now cakes accompanying the coffee as the staff perform their handover. It is with a sense of disbelief that you overhear one of the girls whining on about having had a stressful day; the card machine was playing up and she'd spilt tea on the rota. You hope she chokes on her jam doughnut and then guiltily banish the thought almost immediately because they really, truly, have *no* idea!

A merry jingle of the keys just to remind them you are here and that the rooms are done is rewarded with an air of indifference, but you smile regardless, because it's worth keeping on the right side of the reception staff for reasons I will explain later.

Back into the accursed laundry you scuttle finding a renewed burst of energy, because despite being swallowed up by the steam and the gloom, the end is finally in sight;

Press, press, fold, fold, pile, pile, the last lot of washing is in the machines and we've had the last out of the dryers - for now. There's still turn-down to do yet, and in order to keep on top of the endless mountains of towels and sheets, you will be back in here later like a hamster on a treadmill later. So who is on turn-down tonight?

All eyes swivel my way with avid expectation. Ah, it's me then and my heart drops like a stone. But there's no way out, it's got to be done and it's my turn.

We shuffle out into the golden light of what has been a beautiful day and lift our faces gratefully to the sun as we amble down to the staff car park. The breeze feels good, the air smells sweet. I thank everyone for their hard work with promises to see them on the morrow. It has been a gruelling day but we'll have a few hours of freedom in which to shower, eat and perhaps catch some sleep.

Anyone who has worked split shifts will know that apart from putting small children down the mines and up chimneys, this work pattern has to be one of the cruellest and most unnecessary forms of abuse. There is something infinitely sadistic about being made to work a full day and then totter home knowing you have to go back, especially when you've been up since before dawn and are simply exhausted. But what makes it worse in this case, is that you have to go back and *faff!*

Whoever stole the idea of turning-down beds for the night from the aristocracy should be chained in a laundry room and made to wash everything by hand!

Has there ever been anything so pretentious and unnecessary

in the hospitality trade apart from a waiting-on personage taking your napkin before flicking it out across your lap. Such faff and fuss just for the sake of providing a snobbish and outdated service has always been beyond me and the cause of much resentment.

So back we go, a definite drag in the step as you haul yourself back up the steps and into the lobby. First stop is the laundry room because laundry is king, remember? With weary arms you transfer more mountains of linen into the dryers and then go in search of whoever is in charge that night for the list.

Some guests may not be dining and will be having a tray in their room and will just want clean towels. Another might be enjoying some chill-out time and doesn't want to be disturbed.

In the evening the hotel has taken on a whole different ambience. Glamorous guests gather in the bar before dinner as the serving staff scrape and hover with menu's and canapés. There is candlelight and atmosphere, an air of cultured relaxation and a cooing of voices as everyone is looked after and spoiled to oblivion.

Delicious smells waft out from the kitchens and you can hear the chink of cutlery in the restaurant as staff add the final touches for the night ahead. It's all very nice and urbane and you look longingly at the spare seats in the corner wishing you could be a part of it.

The duty manager is glaring at you; you take the proffered list, it's time to get to work.

I use that term loosely.

Turning back the sheets just-so on a bed you made earlier fills you with no sense of achievement, believe me. Neither does swilling bubbles down the plug-hole and checking there are enough toilet rolls. They've only just checked in that day, for heaven's sake! But you go through the motions,

room to room, draw the curtains, light the lamps, turn down
the bed, leave the chocolates, tidy the bathroom as you
valiantly try not to think how you could be sat down at home
with a nice glass of red or else having a meal with friends.
You open the door after giving the requisite knock-knock
pause, knock-knock and are met with a pair of soft brown
eyes and a thumping tail. Someone has brought their dog for
the night. That's fine; we're hound-friendly here but no, I
wouldn't go in if I were you.

I know the dog looks okay and would probably let you in
with no fuss, but there could be a problem when it's time to
get out. The fact you are going about your business and have
every right to be here is irrelevant; the dog doesn't
understand that, only that you've just stepped into its space
and well...

I can see that you don't believe me – Ok, then let me tell you
a quick story; one night a hapless housekeeper doing turn-
downs came across a dog in a room and was greeted in such
a friendly fashion she thought she'd be alright to go in and
carry out her duties. This she duly did and all was well, until
it was time to leave.

The dog took umbrage at her intent and prevented her from
doing so by adopting such an aggressive manner she was
trapped for over two hours until the owners returned. No one
had missed her, of course.

Once turn-down was done you slipped away into the night
on the unspoken understanding that nobody wants a scrubber
hanging round for longer than was necessary – and to be
honest, someone scuttling about in a cleaning bib hardly
adds to the evening glamour. And so then there was this poor
woman who had to hold on to not just her nerve, but also her
bladder, held hostage by a growling dog.

Ah, I can see you have stepped back. Good. We will not be
turning down this room tonight, so let us just close the door

and let sleepy dogs lie, eh...

Just a few more rooms and then we're done. What's that you say the haunted parts? Yes, they too, have to be done; just don't think about what happened in the attics and you'll be okay, but first back to the laundry with the wet towels. Some guests are happy to re-use them and will hang them out to dry; others will make it clear they want fresh by slinging anything they want replaced in the bath tub, oh, and before we go please put the top back on that toothpaste, as it is the finishing touches that make all the difference, so if you wouldn't mind...I know, I know...

More sorting of the laundry and we're just about done. As we're going through the lobby we're intercepted by the duty manager.

'Bubbles!' he says, and there's a glint in his eyes that tells me he's not best pleased.

I raise an eyebrow, I am genuinely clueless to what it is he is on about, and judging by the look on your face you are, too. He lowers his brow and fixes me with a fierce look that tells me quite clearly I've f****d up!

'Room 12, you haven't rinsed the bath properly. There are still...*bubbles!*'

He spits the last word as though it is something dirty and I detach myself for a moment as the ridiculousness of that statement sinks in. I also take the opportunity to *take him in*. As a rule our paths don't cross very often, he's one of the ones you want to avoid, and the fact he's even deigned to speak to me is quite something in itself and he is obviously affronted.

We stand before him bemused and confused as to where this is going because he is now waiting as though for a suitable response.

I remain clueless, I lift my shoulders. What do you say to that? What does he *expect me to say!*

Seeing that there was going to be no answer forthcoming, his brow now becomes positively thunderous and he snarls, 'Get back to Room 12, you'll need to do it again and this time use *cold water!*'

I think my jaw actually drops open at this point. That he, that *anyone* could be so angry over something so petty was beyond me. That and the fact he'd clearly been going behind us checking our work! I'm now so detached from what's unfolding as to be practically floating in space.

I'm tired. It's been a long day. Dusk is now settling in and I want to go home. If the existence of a few bubbles is so important, so offensive, *so* infuriating to him – why on earth didn't he just turn on the cold water and swish them down himself!

This observation hovers on my lips. I want to put this question to him, I really do, but I can see he's on the verge of *bubble-mania* and clearly a man on the edge. Whether its personal problems, work-related stress, or he's just being a knob, I don't know. But I do know, and with all my heart that if I open my mouth and the words come out he'll go off into the stratosphere and I'll be down the road.

I drop my eyes; my shoulders slump and I turn around and go back for the keys with the air of one making their final walk to the gallows. The unfairness of the situation strikes me and I know you feel it, too, but he is the boss and if he wants to wage war on some bubbles in a bath-tub then let him have his victory tonight because every dog will have its day.

By the time the offending orbs of soapy air have been despatched down the drain and we've returned to the keys to the office, our tormenter is at the desk bidding some guests an obsequious goodnight. It's like theatre and as soon as they're out of sight the mask slips and we are now treated to the frosty face as he snaps,' All done?'

We nod, like the brow-beaten beasts we are and shuffle towards the doors almost expecting to be called back on some other ridiculous pretext or another. But he lets us go with the slightest smirk as you realise that the whole saga of 'Bubblegate' was nothing more than a soap opera and purely of his own doing and for no other reason than he could! I don't know about you but I'm wishing all manner of nasty things upon that balding head and think it a shame he didn't go poking his nose in the room with the dog in it!

But as the saying goes, tomorrow is another day, and so with this thought in mind we'll just crack on because tomorrow all of the guests are checking out, and although it means another busy day, there are only a couple coming in but that means there's a light at the end of the tunnel.

Firstly, however, I'm going to have to run you through a pitch and requisite demeanour designed to break the hardest heart. I mentioned earlier, did I not, about keeping on the right side of reception? Well, let's get the days drudge out of the way and then watch the scene unfold.

As you must have gathered by now, one day is much like another with some more exhausting than others. In days of yore, how house servants coped with 16 hour days I'll never know; and here we are bemoaning an 8 hour shift, but at least we have two days off a week – oftimes they laboured a full seven!

Yes, I know you've had enough of humping laundry but count yourself lucky you're on the final morning, the wheels haven't fallen off the hoover, and the discs in your back are still in place. Come on, keep going, we're nearly there. Just keep your head down and be careful not to glare at reception as we pass as it looks as though they've got cream scones today, in fact, it's probably better that you don't look at all. Ok, we're on the home-run; we'll be out of here by four. Just keep stripping and humping, hoovering and scrubbing. Never mind that stain on the sheets, deal with it, sh*t happens! Oh and don't forget to give an extra spray in this one, it still pongs a bit and get the brush back out on that toilet, would you? You can't leave it looking like *that!*

I can sense your relief as the last room is done and dusted, and we carry the last lot of linen down and feed them into the maws of the ever-hungry machines. The dryers are still going and you wonder, for the umpteenth time, what the electricity bills must be like. But the management have opted for in-house laundry despite the unspoken fact we'd give up our right arm, and gladly, for an outside contractor to take on the load.

With the final sheet folded and piles of napkins neatly pressed, we leave the towels to their tumbling fate because they're the least hassle and can wait until the morning, I hope!

It all depends on whether you can persuade reception to take care of this evening's turn-downs and all will now rest on how pathetic you can be in your quest to get out of it.

Now before we go into the office with the keys, be sure to adopt an exhausted air and a particularly hang-dog expression; a vague kind of faraway look in the eyes also helps, as though you're about to pass out or something.

What do you mean you don't have to pretend? Good, that's even better! You go in front of me and flop about a bit and I'll do the *spiel.*

The two girls on reception duty are deep in discussion when we sidle in and barely notice our entrance. Sundays are the quietest time once lunch is over in most hotels and they've settled in for the 'graveyard' shift with little more to occupy them than garibaldi biscuits and gossip.

At this point a jingling of the keys to announce our presence would merely irritate and get things off on a bad foot, so I

emit a feeble but very politely executed 'ahem' instead.
They chatter on. I clear my throat more loudly and by the
time they both turn around I've assumed 'the position'.
Standing, but only partially erect and with a definite slump.
The eyes are weary, the mouth slack and I maintain this pose
for a couple of seconds so as to have the maximum effect
before quavering in a high reedy voice, 'We're all done,
we'll be off now...'
Their response is vague and disinterested. The housekeepers
are done for the day. Big deal! You can almost hear their
thoughts as they turn back to their coffee and each other.
'But....'
They turn back with an air of impatience. We all know
what's coming. As I said before, it's like theatre. We play
the part of the underdog; they the lofty work-colleagues, and
so we play out the scene as we do most weekends, but the
finale always rests on what mood they're in and their
performance so far isn't encouraging
They're both looking at us much with as much warmth as the
White Witch did at Edmund when he rocked up at her
Winter palace. I slump a little more.
'As there are only two rooms in tonight I was wondering
if...'
I trail off as one of them narrows her eyes and my heart
stops in anticipation of a blank refusal.
I drop my gaze so that she cannot see the rising anger in
mine. It looks as though someone will have to come in for
the sake of half an hour just so some pampered guests can
have their curtains pulled and a few mints left on the pillow.
It wouldn't be so bad but the hotel is miles out in the
countryside so we're talking a 20 mile round trip, and as
Head Housekeeper and all-round mug I know that it'll
probably be me.
There is a pregnant pause and I hang my head as though all

hope is gone before hearing the magic words!
'Oh alright, just this once!' and then they both turn back to
more important matters as you all but skip out of reception
sudden feathers for your feet! Joy threatens to overwhelm
you so great is the relief and you giggle like schoolgirls as
you make your way down the car park with light and happy
hearts!
Tonight there will be no turn-down. Just a nice long relax
and even better, the day off tomorrow. Just before we bid
each other goodnight, I don't mind telling you that the sheer
volume of work in that place had seen off stronger souls
than I, and with no intention of becoming martyr to the mop,
I quit shortly afterwards and two stone lighter!

Thankfully there have been less gruelling jobs and cleaning
in private houses is without a doubt one of them. Laundry is
minimal and you're generally treated with respect. Take the
young mum for instance whose husband was a barrister and
who couldn't do housework because it gave her migraines.
An unusual excuse and a new one on me, but our place is not
to question. So I'd dust and polish around the immaculate
house, she'd be entertaining her young daughter whose room
I dreaded the most.
Not because it was messy, awkward or even particularly
dirty in any way; it was the army of tiny porcelain animals
and I had to dust each and every bloody one. As soon as I
stepped over that threshold my heart would plummet. Not as
tedious as endless piles of laundry, granted, but after a while
it became soul-destroying. There are only so many times you
can buff a badger, polish a penguin, clean a cat before you
seriously consider that perhaps it was this particular part of
the housekeeping that triggered my boss's migraines – that
or the threat of developing the screaming heebie-jeebies!
I could stand it no more and mumbled some excuse over the

phone about an allergy to house dust before going to clean for a retired Jewish couple instead.

They didn't have an army of ornaments, indeed they even took care of their own laundry; but they had a houseful of venetian blinds, and a rabid aversion to them gathering even so much as a speck of dust! As I wiped each one meticulously with a slightly damp cloth, I told myself over and over that it was worth it because they treated me like one of the family and happily paid above the going rate. They would also insist I sat and had coffee with them whilst the wife served home-made honey cakes. It was one of the nicest and easiest cleaning jobs I ever had, but the blinds got to me in the end so I moved on.

Boredom can be the biggest killer when you've got hours of monotony before you dispelled only by talking to the mop. How else do you while away the time as you plough through the same chores day after day?

It is my belief that solitary acts of scrubbing develop an innate need to engage in *all* manner of conversations; particularly with yourself.

My favourite was to pretend I was being interviewed as I went about my work. By jabbering away with what and why and how I was doing something certainly filled the time and was a way of trying to instil some interest in the daily slog. This is all very well and good until you get caught.

That's bad enough, but imagine holding forth whilst employing two different voices as you service a room in the belief it is empty. Hearing the toilet flush in the ensuite is akin to a volcanic eruption as you realise with unmitigated horror that your little *tete a tete* has been overheard in its entirety, and that whoever has been tucked away in the bathroom has obviously been waiting for *you* to leave so they can come out!

I mean, it's one thing to emerge from your ablutions with just the housekeeper, indeed that could even be regarded as acceptable; but to have to come out and face *two* women conducting some kind of interview in your room is a whole different kettle of fish and I was understandably mortified. Because not only did I have to pass the bathroom in order to exit the room, but the bathroom door was actually beginning to open which meant the 'mystery' guest would see quite clearly that I was quite alone and with a possible diagnosis of split personality.

It was one of those situations where you simply want the floor to open up and swallow you whole, and as I sidled towards the door my cleaning tray held before me, this poor bloke came out and proceeded to look beyond me with a slightly puzzled look on his face. Blushing furiously I kept going as I babbled my apologies with the promise I would call back later.

I still squirm when I think of that moment, and can only imagine the impression it must have made on him. Thankfully he said nothing but he never came back and I'm sure he too, has a story to tell of that morning. Suffice to say I kept a very low profile until he checked out and made it a rule never to engage with the 'voices' unless I knew for sure that the coast was clear.

The turd in the bed – and I know you haven't forgotten about that! – came along some years later in a small guest house whose main customer base were contractors from all over. For the most part servicing rooms for such *clientele* would be as varied as they were. Indeed I have been surprised more than once by the extreme neatness of some contractors who have grafted on building sites all day, as by those suited and booted to such a high standard you'd find it hard to associate that person with the squalor they'd leave behind.

One guest particularly springs to mind. Immaculately groomed and smelling like heaven at breakfast, my shock after he'd checked out and I saw the state of his room was unparalleled. Sweet wrappers, crisps and half-eaten snacks strewn in and around the bed; fag-ends and rubbish just dropped and left and, the most disgusting of all – urine in the sink because he'd been too lazy to use the bathroom. An excellent example of how appearances can lie!

The turd in the bed, however, exceeded all prior unpleasant surprises and I'm not sure the poor housekeeper who found it ever got over it!

Hearing my name screeched with great distress I flew expecting some great catastrophe but was suitably shocked upon being presented with a long skinny length of excrement lying snugly upon the bottom sheet.

Babbling, the housekeeper told me that she was making the bed when there it was, like some long brown snake caught napping. We stared at it and then at each other and I could see she was upset. I, however, was more intrigued.

How on earth can you crap in your bed in your sleep and then somehow extricate yourself the next morning without disturbing it? Unless he was caught mid-dump whilst half-asleep and decided to let nature takes its course anyway. But then why would anyone want to do that? How anyone they leave such an obnoxious offering for some poor young girl to find.

We were flabbergasted. It took the expression of not *giving a sh*t* to a whole new level!

The pooping perpetrator was due back that night and someone had to tell him. I didn't envy the manager this task but she said he took it calmly and that she felt, ironically, the whole exchange had been more embarrassing for her than for him. And it wasn't long before we found out why when he pooped in the bed the *next night*. This time we were up in arms!

Surely he must've known? Surely you cannot crap in the bed
two nights in a row and not *know* about it! We were as
bewildered as we were furious. Cleaning up after other
peoples' shite was one thing, but this was a turd too far!!
There was only one thing for it and the manager didn't
hesitate. He may have checked out that morning never to
return. But we had his company details and none were
spared our end as the manager enlightened them as to their
employee's dirty bed-time habit and that he was banned
forthwith ever to darken our door again, never mind the bed
linen!

She allowed us to listen in on speaker-phone. I'm guessing
she felt our outrage was entitled to that much. To hear the
bewildered apology after the shocked silence was worth it
alone - as was the knowledge serial pooper had been busted
and now seriously in the sh*t! (Pun intended).

My mind touched on all of the housemaids over the
centuries, hundreds of thousands of them, millions even, and
how they had to deal with such nastiness and without
complaint.

How lucky are we that we can demand redress and shame the
dirty dumpers who have no respect for those who clean up
after them? And how lovely it is when you'd find a small
note thanking you for your efforts, and sometimes, if you're
lucky a nice little tip. Just ensure you hand it in because you
never know when your trustworthiness will be tested and any
scrubber worth their salt should be nothing less than squeaky
clean.

And so here endeth our little foray into the upstairs
downstairs world of hotel housekeeping. The largely unseen
but extremely hard-working army of modern-day
maidservants pandering to the paying masses so we can

enjoy the fruits of their labours.

So spare a thought the next time you slip between the cool crisp sheets knowing that the only surprise you're going to find in that bed is nothing chocolatey than a mint crisp, and that you have the wonderful forbearance of the scrubber to thank for that.

TO COOK OR NOT TO COOK

How on earth I fell into the culinary side of hospitality is still a mystery to me, and there have been few steeper learning curves than my foray into the food quarter, and as usual there is someone to blame for it!

I could cook, yes. Rustle up the usual stuff like Spag Bol, a Roast, Home-made chips and bake the odd crumble. Even when I ran establishments cooking breakfasts for 24+ it was hardly rocket science and microwave ovens took care of the rest.

I liked to think I was quietly capable on a very basic level and never aspired to be anything more than a kitchen mechanic who'd never gone any further than the first year - until I was put forward for a job by someone whose faith in my cooking abilities exceeded my own.

Picture the scene, if you will, a rambling old house high up in the hills that has views to die for. It's an activity centre that plays host to various youth clubs and is staffed by overseas students.

Initially I'm intrigued and envisage nothing more challenging than sausage and chips with the occasional trifle thrown in. But oh, how wrong was I!

And how sly were they as the full facts of the job were

glossed over like fine icing as I found myself being cajoled into position. The money was great; they were appealing and I was flattered to be offered the job on the spot.

As I was shown into my new work-place my mind was still full of fat-fryers and fishfingers and I all but keeled over with shock.

This was no cosy cottage kitchen. Before me was a proper-jobby, the real deal, an industrial-sized kitchen with massive saucepans stacked along one work surface and a humongous cooker with no less than three ovens!

I blanched. Surely they couldn't be serious! Little ol' egg-frying me - take charge of this lot?

As I took it all in a sample menu was waved before me and my eyes widened further.

Soup, lasagne, chilli, pizza; no big deal, you're thinking, but everything had to be home-made right down to the base pastry - and then there was the dessert list and I positively quailed before *that!* Sponges, pies, tarts and – the most terrifying of all, *homemade chocolate sauce!*

I practically passed out on the spot.

Surely not? No way! I could just about cobble a cheese one together, never mind a *chocolate!*

I gave a greasy grin and turned to the nice couple with barely-suppressed panic in my eyes and came clean.

'Look, it's really kind of you to have offered me the job, and it's a lovely place and everything, but I really don't think I'm up to the task. You need someone more experienced. *Much* more experienced!'

They smiled back at me indulgently and waved their hands airily.

'Oh don't you worry about that. You'll have Christina to help. She knows how everything works, you'll be fine, Mandy.'

'No, really...'

'We're *so* looking forward to having you on-board and as poor Christina has been having to do it *all* herself, she will be *absolutely* over the moon!'

In the face of such enthusiasm I trailed off; they had me and they knew it. My concerns having been so adroitly dismissed and with no further arguments forthcoming, I suddenly found myself a Cook!

In something of a dazed state I turned up the next day for work to find the angel who was Christina, waiting to show me the ropes.

And they weren't wrong. She did know everything as far as that kitchen was concerned, but because she was a volunteer she wasn't allowed to take up the position officially. Suffice to say, she became both my left and my right arm and sometimes my brain.

Knowing I had her unstinting support I began to relax with the tentative hope that perhaps I'd be up to the job; the proof would be in the pudding and I, who had never created anything more exotic than a sherry trifle would soon discover!

A group of children would soon be arriving for a two-night stay, but in the meantime I'd be cooking just for the five staff. The clock was ticking, however and I needed to get cracking. Straight after the interview and my somewhat forced acceptance, I had hot-footed it down to see the friend who had put me forward.

'Don't worry,' she had cooed soothingly, 'you'll be fine. Here, you can borrow this if you're that worried.'

I looked up and she was holding out a small brown book. It was a cook book by a well-known food-goddess and I grabbed at it like a drowning woman.

A quick flick through showed me nothing more frightening than a comprehensive guide to basic home cooking and I began to calm down. Between this little brown bible and Christina I could do this, as long as I stuck to the script and didn't get fancy.

During that first shift it soon became apparent that the House Mother was well into recycling when I was asked to make vegetable soup using all of the leftovers. Peering into the humungous fridge I pulled out the arse-end of all manner of greenery but my hand hesitated over a certain vegetable and I looked around at her questioningly.

'Yes, all of them, please,' she said, 'Christina will be here soon. I'll leave you to it.'

Duly I made up some stock and began to chop and then add bits of carrot, celery, onion and cabbage but I still couldn't get my head around that one vegetable and as soon as Christina came in I waved it at her like it was some kind of voodoo doll I'd found in the cupboard.

'She wants me to put *this* in the soup! Do I put it in? I mean, *really?* '

The young woman tried to suppress a smile and I knew I must have cut a comical figure but I didn't want to fall so spectacularly at the first fence. *I had to be sure!*

'Yes,' she replied unconcernedly, 'Just chop it up and put it in.'

By the time the staff turned up to receive their lunch I was in a veritable sweat. It just didn't seem *right*, and I was convinced I'd be laughed out the door as soon as my concoction was put before them. This was because the soup was *purple* on account of the beetroot everyone insisted I put in it! This was my first culinary offering and obviously I wanted to make a good impression, but *purple soup!*

So it was with great trepidation as I ladled this colourful creation into the bowls as Christina took out the bread. All staff ate together, including the House Parents and as a rule, the bogus cook, but I insisted I wasn't hungry and hid in the kitchen peeping through the hatch instead.

I watched with growing dread as Christina placed the bowls before them and was amazed to see just the one eyebrow go up - not in displeasure, but more in pleasant surprise and I stopped breathing.

No one said a word. They just picked up their spoons and got stuck in as I hovered like a culinary ghoul in anticipation of extreme exorcism.

It didn't come. They just carried on eating and talking about the centre, so I decided to further my luck and sidled in through the door.

'Is everything...okay?'

My voice sounded too high-pitched to my ears but I was rewarded by five beaming faces as they all turned round to look at me and thank me for the lovely soup.

The lovely soup! Seriously?

I looked from one to the other. Surely they were having a laugh. Who, in all honesty, could sit down to something like that and not be offended! I was strangely perplexed. It was all just so surreal.

After they'd left I turned to Christina with all the earnestness of one who had just discovered that the earth was flat, and asked how anyone could possibly *not* be offended by being served purple soup - it really was quite beyond me.

'It wouldn't matter if it had been black!' she cried delightedly, 'we have a *cook* and that's all that matters!'

'No, you *think* you have a cook. Christina, I have basic cooking skills and just reading the menu for the week is enough to send me running for the hills! Roast chicken dinner for forty? I've only ever done six! It's too much, I'm telling you, and I'm also expected to bake cakes – *cakes, for crying out loud!'*

My anguish was almost palpable and coming across
Christina laid a comforting hand on my arm. Even to this
day I still believe she was some kind of angel.
'It's okay, don't worry. I will help you. We will do this
together.'

And so began my foray into the frightening world of feeding
the masses without poisoning them, and under Christina's
calm tutelage soon I was banging out all manner of culinary
delights and a chocolate sauce not to be sniffed at!
Of the latter, no one was more surprised than me, and I have
Della, the domestic goddess to thank for that and the
celestial Christina, of course!
I was doing okay, there were no disasters and soon I was
wrangling those saucepans and operating equipment like an
old-kitchen hand! Having recently become a vegetarian I
managed to get around this by mouthing whatever meat
concoction was on the menu before spitting it out.
Fortunately this was enough to appease my bosses who had
not been willing with my initial proposal of just having a
sniff.
I was far from happy about this but we all must bend with
the wind and back in the day I was nothing less than
flexible. I had gained so much confidence in by pushing the
boundaries but the shift patterns were a killer and something
had to give.
At the height of the season I would be in for breakfast, back
for lunch, and then back again for dinner which meant I was
burning petrol - and myself out at one hell of a rate.
Admittedly the money was good, but a decision had to be
made and my life had become that kitchen. I marvelled at
those who chose to do this as a living because after a few
months I'd had enough. This whole kitchen-mechanic thing
wasn't really for me. Working split shifts was one thing, but

having to do treble was another.

I could see why they had problems recruiting never mind retaining a full-time cook. The hours were crippling and they expected a lot. Even with Christina at my side I'd had enough of working in a hot environment. Cue the old adage 'If you can't stand the heat, get out of the kitchen' and so I did - literally!

If you think that was quick my next cooking job lasted the grand total of two days. Again I was lured by the money. A life in service, no matter the position unless you're the top of your game is notoriously badly-paid. It's also sheer slog for very little gain and pay on a par with peanuts.

So if an opportunity presents itself for better working conditions, sometimes you've just got to go for it in the hope your skill set will allow for success.

But back to the job; the pay was good, the hours not bad and the numbers to cook for pretty static. The fact I needed to mull it over for a couple of days should have been a warning sign; indecisiveness, I have since learnt, often goes hand in hand with low-level intuition.

The position was in a secure unit for people with behavioural problems – some more acute than others – and I would be cooking on average for no more than thirty people. The place itself was darkly daunting with a touch of the old Gothic. It had probably once been a lovely family home to some prosperous merchant, but faded grandeur was all that was left of its past. The rooms were stark and deliberately so. No pictures or ornaments, just chairs and sofas and a large TV.

The interview has gone well and much reassurance given that there would be no danger. I would be locked in the kitchen at all times and no client would ever have access with, or without their carers except for David.

David was one of the more stable residents who enjoyed
helping out in the kitchen. He was a quiet man with a
diagnosis of paranoid schizophrenia and had been at the unit
for many years. *There's nothing to worry about,* they told
me, *we trust him and it's important he continues to feel
useful. Did I have a problem with that?*
No, not really, but I would prefer to reserve judgment until I
had met him.
It was with an almost sense of disappointment when I got a
call to say I got the job, and that should have been my
warning. But money talks, or in this case sings like a siren
from the rocks and despite my uneasiness I turned sail and
went in...

My first stint was with the other cook, Sian, who was bright
and breezy and very efficient. She showed me around,
including the root cellar where all dry goods were kept and
warned me never to leave the key in the door. I must ensure
that I kept that, and the kitchen key on me at *all* times.
Her words sent a shiver down my back. The fact the place
was so old and creepy didn't help. Coupled with my age-old
fear of cellars, I also didn't like the idea of being locked in.
I felt as though I was my own jailer, it was an extraordinary
work situation, but then as the day went on I could see why.
The house was noisy and busy. Many of the clients liked to
move about, their carers close on their heels, and often
you'd hear them before you'd see them and their distress at
times was quite voluble and hard to bear.
And then there was David. Small, stocky, late fifties and
with an air of nervousness that didn't bode well. This
became apparent when Sian introduced us and he refused to
shake my hand. He drew back as though I might infect him
and averted his eyes. Not a great start. He obviously felt
unsure of me, but I understood enough to know that this was

a part of his condition and that it would take time.

It soon became evident that not only did he trust Sian but that he absolutely adored her. When she allocated him a job he set to with all the devotion of an obedient dog, and when she unlocked a drawer and handed him a knife I felt my eyes widen and she noticed immediately.

'Oh, it's alright.' she said brightly, 'David always has access to the knives. He's the only one who does but we trust him.'

Two things struck me here and simultaneously; firstly that she spoke about him as though he wasn't there, and secondly, I was alarmed that such implements were accessible to a client who was, to all intents and purposes, still considered ill enough to be living in a secure unit.

I held my tongue and carried on with the food prep, but inwardly I was far from happy. I couldn't help the odd surreptitious glance in David's direction who was equally keeping an eye on me as he chopped cabbages.

'They have the main meal at lunchtime,' Sian explained, 'and sandwiches with cake for tea. Today they'll be having meat and two veg – all except for Charlie who has the same thing every day, so make sure it's on the table or else he'll kick off if he doesn't get it.'

I swallowed. 'Oh?'

'Jacket spud with cheese and beans, twice a day, every day. So whatever you do, make sure you always throw a few in the oven or there'll be trouble. And for pudding today,' she breezed on, 'they'll be having Jam roly poly with custard.'

I mentally consulted Della in my head as I measured out the ingredients for the sponge. David had now finished the veg and was stood by the sink having a cup of tea and I felt him watching me.

I looked up and smiled but his eyes slid away and I was very aware the knife drawer was still unlocked. More worrying still was the sense that not only did he not like me - but that he didn't *want* to like me, and there was absolutely nothing I could do about that. I moved position so as to be nearer the door and then nearly jumped out of my skin as a sudden loud bang came from it.

I spun round and caught a glimpse of a shaggy-haired giant who glared in at me and gave a great roar before lumbering off. Two male carers scuttled after him and well rattled I turned and looked at Sian.

'That's Charlie!' She said cheerfully.

Lunch was an interesting affair and seemed to go well. To my relief David had gone to join the other residents and I watched them through the hatch as they tucked in, but my eyes kept going back to the one called Charlie who was making short work of his jacket potatoes.

He was *huge!* His carers, half his size but still quite burly watched him much as you'd watch a drowsing tiger and I admired their calm demeanour as I did the rest of the staff who were obviously dedicated to a difficult job

I had allowed myself to become distracted and now the custard had gone all lumpy. I grimaced with embarrassment, this wasn't good, *and* on my first day. I made my apologies.

'No, don't worry, lumpy custard is *good.*'

'It is?' For the second time that morning I assumed the look of someone who had just fallen down the rabbit hole.

'Oh yes,' Sian went on, 'we're not here to serve perfectly prepared food as you would in a restaurant. We want the clients to feel as though they're having *real* food as they would do at home. So if there are lumps in the custard then believe me, that's absolutely fine!'

I was rather perplexed by this explanation, but on the other hand I could see the reasoning behind it – to a degree. I could also see that there were a lot of aspects to this position that would require a rapid mind-expansion. David having

access to the knife drawer being just one of them, and I aired
my concerns.
'I understand what you're saying, but honestly, you have
nothing to worry about. David's been here for years and has
always helped out in the kitchen. He's just suspicious of you
because he doesn't know you, that's all. Give him a couple
of weeks and he'll soon settle down.'
A couple of weeks!
I left that day feeling extremely uncomfortable with the
whole set-up. A close family member had worked in mental
health for years and I was no stranger to it, so it was with no
small misgivings I arrived for my first shift the next morning
to find David waiting outside the kitchen.
I greeted him in a cordial fashion. Not too much, not too
little he mumbled something but still wouldn't look at me.
The day passed slowly and I soon realised that no amount of
chatter, witty asides, or spring-like smiles would induce him
to offer anything more in return than a nod and we eyed each
other covertly throughout the shift.
Prep went well and the food went out and I had all the
knives back in the drawer as soon as was feasibly possible.
But the atmosphere was taut and I knew he was on
tenterhooks as much and that couldn't be good for both of
us. Indeed I had never known such an odd working
environment and I didn't know if I'd be able to hack it.
The decision was made for me later that evening at home
when I finally found the time to read through the induction
pack I'd been issued end of shift.

Now most places would, and should, give you some form of
induction before starting any job and in this position
especially so. But the powers-that-be had been crafty and
had thrown me on board knowing full well that if I'd been in
possession of the full facts, I'd have equally as quickly

thrown myself *off!*

Now just to be clear, I have no problem with people with mental health issues and due to my family's affiliation in this field, I probably have more understanding than most. Indeed I went on to work in this sector years later. But it is only fair to give new employees the *full* picture before they enter into *any* work environment that has potential risks.

I understood that finding a counter-part to the unflappable Sian had probably not been an easy task, and so they'd neatly side-stepped procedure by presenting me with a whole dossier on the client base and what not to do *after* I'd accepted the job!

As I read through extremely personal and confidential reports I could feel the hair on the back of my neck rising. I also wondered why I'd been given access to such sensitive information when I was just the cook, for heaven's sake! It just didn't seem right. Then I came to the part where it said *all* staff were expected to interact with the clients in a bid to encourage socialisation and prevent barriers. The hulking figure of Charlie rose up before my eyes and I knew I'd need more than a barrier if he decided to come at me!

I read on and it was very clear; as the cook, I would also, at times, be expected to step out from the safe confines of the kitchen and have coffee in the lounge, or join them they were eating in order to make myself 'approachable'.

Yes, yes, I could see all that and the reasoning behind it, but then did I really want to chance being put into a headlock whereby the advice given was not to struggle and to remain calm? Because according to the dossier on this particular client, the more you panicked the tighter he'd squeeze.

Or risk being attacked by one of the clients who hated long hair with the added warning that a neatly-tied bun would be no deterrent. At this point Sian rose in my mind with her short cropped style and I clutched at my long tresses protectively.

By the time I'd finished reading through the spine-chilling manual my mind was made up and I reached for the phone. Banging out lumpy custard was one thing, but having to constantly look over my shoulder was another – especially in the one place that was supposed to be my safe haven.

I made the call and told them they should've been upfront and that I was not willing to stay even if they put me in a space suit and paid me treble!

I was wary after that and steered clear of any cooking jobs. But then subsequent experiences of working in the service industry showed quite clearly that there are those walking around who should be locked up as you'll discover later. For now, let us just leave it as we began; to cook or not to cook? Think you all know my answer to that!

ODDS, SODS AND DASTARDLY DEEDS

No story would be complete without tales of scams and scallywags and unscrupulous dealings, and Lord knows I've had my fair share! Many years after me doing just about every job imaginable in the hotel trade, I was finally given the opportunity to run one myself.

Hotel manager - sounds grand, doesn't it?

But it forgets to mention the plethora of other jobs that you have to do when staff call in sick or simply let you down. It also fails to mention the fact you are the first port of call and line of defence in any given situation, and so you must be savvy and able to stand firm when the ground gets shaky. Being possession of biceps like Popeye would help tremendously, but failing that always have a bloody big stick!

My first experience with an undesirable and distinctly unsavoury customer was when a silver-tongued devil turned up at the door one day and immediately there was something about him I couldn't put my finger on, but business is business and so I let him in.

I had questions, however, the usual pitter-patter when you're checking someone in, and he had an answer for everything. No car? Major problem with the engine, firm sent him down on the train.

Luggage? Somehow went missing on the changeover but the rail company were on to it.

He was very forthcoming about why he was in the area, however, and that he was on a recruitment drive for some 'mining' project up the valleys. His enthusiasm was infectious as explained how he would fill the place with contractors once 'the project' was off the ground, and what an exciting opportunity it would be for local people. I was suspicious, but he was urbane, charming, and I decided to give him the benefit of the doubt.

Hindsight, as I mentioned before, is a marvellous thing, but the business I was running was in competition with at least another dozen on the street, and so despite my misgivings he soon found himself settled in a room on the top floor.

With half an eye I clocked his movements. After breakfast he'd be out all day, sometimes not returning until early evening and often with a takeaway that he'd usually offer to share. A guest offering food in this way was a new one on me and aroused my suspicions even more, and then after a week when first payment was due, I presented him with the bill.

Without as much as a pause he looked me right in the eye and said, 'No probs, I'll go up to the hole in the wall and get it now.'

Such aplomb. *Had I been wrong?*

Furtively I watched him as he walked down the hall and out with not so much as a backward glance, and for some reason I had been expecting that, because that's what dodgy people do, right?

But he must've felt my eyes on his back and he was cool, I'll give him that. Straight out of the front door, down the path, and I never clapped eyes on him again.

Upon checking his room later, the possessions he'd left

behind amounted to little more than a few items of clothing and some toiletries. This was a man who travelled light, unhindered by personal effects that may weigh him down – or even more tellingly, compromise his story. We didn't find as much as a scrap of paper to say who he was and where he was from. He had simply walked out that morning like a ghost.

He did, however, leave a trail of destruction in his wake, and the first I knew about this was when some woman who worked at the local laundrette kept calling the hotel wanting to speak to him until sheer desperation finally saw her make a tear-filled confession to me.

Not only had our fine-feathered phoney convinced her that all of his cases had been stolen from the train – along with his wallet - but he had so wooed her into feeling so sorry for him she handed over *all* of her Christmas savings, including the monies her daughter had left with her for safe-keeping.

I was aghast. Her self-flagellation was pitiful. I was also furious at the sheer callousness of what he'd done, but what could I do? The woman had been well and truly stung. I felt for her, but there was nothing I could do other than advise her to go to the police. It went without saying he was long gone and I thought that was the last of it until I was having coffee a few mornings later with one of the cleaners when we received a surprise visit.

Most guests used the front door, unless they parked up in the back when entry would then be made via the bar. Hearing a car pulling up, idly I wondered who could be back so early when I suddenly saw two angry-looking men coming at speed towards the back door wielding baseball bats.

For a brief moment I thought I was seeing things and then they were in and before us like two raging before coming to an abrupt halt the bats held threateningly.

What made it even more frightening was that the cleaner had her two year old daughter with her and that scared me more than anything else. These guys were on a no-nonsense mission and had obviously come to rob the place.

This was no time for the 10ft Amazonian woman. Releasing her would have served only to exacerbate the situation so I remained calm and asked them what they wanted.

'Him! Where is he?' the one snarled with barely suppressed fury and I stared back blankly. I had expected a demand for the till or the safe and was completely thrown of course.

'Him..?'

He waved the bat before me menacingly, 'Don't piss me about! You know who I mean! *Him!* That smooth-talking bastard you're shagging!'

'What?' I gasped.

'You know! That f*cking Geordie! Where the f*ck is he? *We're going to kill him!'*

The penny dropped and so did my jaw.

'WHAT! That cheeky fat git said he was shagging *me?'*

Now it was my turn to be outraged and I could feel my cheeks flush with fury. The 10 ft Amazonian Woman stirred and I had a job to keep her down.

'Believe me, if he was still here I'd take the bat from you and do it myself and gladly, because not only has he done a runner on *me!* But he also ripped off some poor woman and all her Christmas savings for her grandkids! He's gone. He went last Friday when I asked him to pay up!'

It was as though my words pulled a plug and you could see all the adrenaline start to seep out of these guys as it dawned on them that we had all been had.

They lowered the bats slowly, almost sheepishly. They believed me. *Thank God!*

It turned out he'd been extremely busy around the local pubs – courtesy of that poor woman's money, no doubt! He had

enticed a number of young men looking for work into believing he could sort them with the kind of pay they could only dream of. What his firm really needed, he told them, was drivers and he'd persuaded several into handing over their driving licenses with the promise he'd return them as soon as... and well, you can guess the rest.
Fortunately nothing more was damaged other than these young bucks' pride, not to mention the trusting nature of a goodly soul. But it had been a terrifying lesson so when the next conman tried to strike I was ready for him!

Had I met this individual at the door in the first instance, just his appearance alone would have got the old alarm bells jingling and when he opened his mouth it was even worse.
I'd come back from an evening off to find him holding forth at the top of his voice in the bar
Turning to the staff member I'd left in charge I hissed, 'Who or what - on earth is *this?*'
It was more of a demand than a question as I took in the tall rangy figure, the shabby suit, the shock of red hair and the loud hectoring tones that were emitted in a broad London accent.
'I don't know. I booked him in earlier.'
'For how long? And did you get the money off him upfront?'
I was mesmerised, I couldn't take my eyes off him. He towered above the rest of the guests who were all looking distinctly uncomfortable. He was like a force of nature but of the most perilous kind. I just knew he was going to be trouble. Big trouble...
'The rest of the week... and er...no'
I gave her my best Medusa-stare and she gazed back slightly perplexed. She really didn't have a clue.
'Okay, you get off, I'll take it from here.'
'But it's your night off you shouldn't have to lock up.'

I turned on her.

'Well it looks like I'm going to have to now, doesn't it! What on earth were you thinking letting *him* in? What have I said about oddbods at the door? We. Do. Not. Let. Them. In!' She squirmed apologetically before making a fast exit and I took position up behind the bar and braced myself. A few of the regular guests looked relieved to see me and made a break mouthing 'Good night' before running for the stairs. Oh dear, not a good sign. Most of these guys were big, burly contractors; hardly flimsy male material but they were visibly intimidated.

I watched my nemesis in action. He was brash, abrasive, the force of his personality wielded like a crudely-honed weapon. A line from the song by *Frankie Goes to Hollywood* 'Two Tribes' came to my mind; *Seek and destroy* and I took a deep breath. This one was going to have to be handled with double-steel gauntlets never mind kid-gloves.

By this time it was nearly midnight I made it clear the bar would be closing. As there were only a couple of guests left at this point judging by their faces there would be no argument from them, he, however...

'Aww...' came a whining voice as the giant and fixed me with what he probably fancied was a little-boy look, but I wasn't having any of it and we locked stares for some moments before he changed tack.

'Oh, so you're the boss, then, are you?'

He said it like it was up for discussion and I gave a brittle smile. My Amazonian counterpart stood quietly by at the ready.

'Yes, I am so if you'd like to take your drink upstairs that's fine, or else see it off, please, because the bar is closing,' I paused for added effect, *'now.'*

I saw his eyes flash but pretended not to notice. I was used to bolshie men and their aversion to assertive women. As I wiped down and washed out the trays he stood silently sipping at his beer. That he was sussing me out, I had no doubt. I could feel his mind all over me like a creeping insect as though seeking a way in. The 'feel' from him was most unpleasant and everyone else had gone. Knights in shining armour come in short supply these days and I had been left me to it.

It was only when I turned out the lights that he finally sloped off chuntering under his breath. This character was really something else, and as I double-locked my door that night I vowed to have him out the next morning.

Breakfast is always a pleasant and sometimes lively part of the day that as a rule I enjoyed immensely. But on this occasion I was filled with apprehension for what I knew had to be done. There was no man or muscle to support me, no beefy side-kick to protect and watch my back – just 5' 5' of Sagittarian determination and I felt like Perseus about to take down the Kraken. Indeed I would never need the 10ft Amazonian Woman more.

Despite the hub-bub of voices in the breakfast room and the radio playing, you could hear his heckling tones from the kitchen. He was informing anyone who cared to listen that he was some kind of high-flying hot-shot. It would've been funny if it hadn't been so untrue. The man was dressed little better than a tramp and had all the finesse of a back-street brawler. There was absolutely no way he would be allowed to stay. He had to go.

I told the waitress that as soon as he had eaten that I wanted a word with him out the back. The 'back' was the bar and where bills were settled up. Anyone else would've seen it coming, but he thought he had his feet so firmly under the table his response when it came was immediately aggressive. Favouring me with his best hectoring tone he barked, 'What

do you mean, I have to leave? I booked this room for the rest of the week! *The girl said I could!'*
'The girl,' I said calmly, 'did not check the diary properly, and as I explained, your room has been reserved for tonight and we have no others available. Again I can only apologise, and I will be speaking to the staff member concerned so this doesn't happen again.'
I pushed the invoice across the bar to him.
'So if you could just settle up and for your bar tab from last night.'
He jutted his considerable jaw out belligerently and snapped, 'I'm not paying *that!'* before deliberately flicking it to the floor.
Had he thrown a glove between us the message couldn't have been any clearer. It was the penultimate challenge and one issued by those who think they can bully their way out of payment. Inwardly I took a deep breath. I wasn't surprised. Not really. But it was going to get nasty before it got better, and with no hero to help take up the battle I now assumed full Amazonian status.
'You'll have to pay. It's *your* bill.'
'I'm not, I'm telling you.'
I raised an eyebrow my voice cool.
'And I'm telling *you*. You can't come wandering into a hotel and expect bed and breakfast for free. What is this? *Who the hell do you think you are?'*
He erupted. Just when I thought those hectoring tones couldn't get any louder he raged and he bawled as he threw himself about in spectacular fashion insisting *there was no way he was going to pay that bill!*
It was one hell of a tantrum, I'll give him that, and so obviously well-practiced I'd have put him forward for an Oscar. But I also knew that if I betrayed any fear by so much as a flicker he'd raise the bar and then I'd be in trouble.

Rant over he paused panting in my face as he fixed me with
those crazy eyes, lips bared like a rabid beast, and I held the
fevered glare stoically as I stared down from my imagined
lofty height.

'You still have to pay the bill.' My words were calmly
delivered with not so much as a quaver and he drew back as
though considering his next move.

We stared at each other and then he surprised me. Instead of
the raging beast, he now turned back to the plaintive tones of
the poor, hapless customer who had been treated *so* unfairly!
So inconvenienced! Treated with *such* disrespect *and*
expected to pay for the privilege! He was a *businessman,*
didn't I know it! A *businessman,* for f*cks sake, and he'd
never been treated like this. *Ever!*

Evidently this was yet another ploy and I could almost feel
sorry for him, such was the belief in his own delusion. As he
held forth, I took in the faded, shiny suit that was too short
on the gangling limbs. The yellowed shirt with a twisted tie
of no known pattern. The scruffy shoes that denoted him
clearly as not someone you'd associate as a mover and
shaker and fleetingly I wondered what his true story was.
The bill still had to be paid, however, and my instincts told
me that if I weakened on that I may not get him out at all.
There was some small room for compromise and perhaps
that would be enough.

I went to interrupt but he was in full flow, his face
increasingly red as he worked himself back up into a frenzy.
Not wanting to take my chances a second time with the fury
of the Kraken I found myself shouting, 'Alright! *Alright!'*
He came up for breath like some fire-breathing dragon all
but spent but hungry for more; and I was a damsel in
distress, not quite Andromeda tied to the rocks but too close
for comfort. Someone had to get this lunatic out!

'Okay!' I said as forcefully as I could, 'We'll forget the bar,

just pay for the room or...' and as he went to open his maw, I
spat, now thoroughly fed up, '*I'll call the bloody police!*'
He considered this as he viewed me with one jaundiced eye.
I cocked an eyebrow in reply. We stared at each other for
some moments then he finally capitulated.
'*Awright.* Well how much is that then!'
I told him and he pulled out a flea-bitten wallet he'd
probably found in a skip, and wordlessly I marvelled at the
bulging wad within. *He was loaded!*
I looked up into his craggy face and glared at him. But now
mission accomplished, he was busy peeling off a couple of
notes seemingly satisfied and I could've wept! But at least
the beast had been appeased and he was soon on his way.
As I watched him stride off down the path I wondered how
many other places he'd pulled the same stunt in, or more
pressing still, where was he heading next? I quickly got on
to the phone to warn my fellow-hoteliers; he'd be lucky to
find a room on this street by the time I'd finished!

Despite being in competition with each other, for the most
part us hoteliers enjoyed cordial relations and generally
looked out for each other. A quick description was all that
was needed before the 'unwanted guest' knocked at the door
only to be told that only a family room was available at
some ridiculously inflated rate that would make even the
most polished con man think twice.
But not all masters of deceit were blithe or aggressive; some
were so incredibly smooth they passed completely beneath
the radar like the elderly Scottish gentleman who booked in
one night. He had come down for his granddaughter's
inauguration at University and he was soooo looking
forward to it! He was soooo proud... As the pay-in advance
system was still loosely applied and he seemed so nice, old
dopey here checked him. His reservation was for two nights

and I was suitably aghast when he failed to show up for breakfast the second morning. A swift reccy of his room revealed nothing more than an old pair of shoes to say he'd ever been there...

I was completely mystified. Who would leave a pair of shoes behind? Where was he? Had he forgotten to take them with him - early stages of dementia perhaps and he *thought* he'd paid? I was keen to grab on to anything to say I hadn't been duped, but in my heart I knew it.

The mystery of the shabby shoes was solved a few days when I saw my local paper. An elderly 'Scottish gentleman' matching his description had gone into a shop, tried on a pair of shoes, and whilst the assistant was distracted simply walked out in them. How could anyone so old and genteel be so crooked? But it takes all kinds, I guess, and I couldn't help but be bemused by his sting. The 'gentleman' was obviously an 'old hand' and it was his meek manner that was his greatest weapon for he could ebb and flow before melting away like Scotch mist. He was without doubt, a true master of the con!

And then we have those who think they can pull a fast one but aren't quite bright enough to see it through. If you're going to wet the bed – twice - either sort yourself out with some incontinence pads or else 'fess up and face the consequences.

Cue two contractors staying in a twin room; housekeeping comes to me, one of them has had an accident and so we pull out the mattress for a deep clean and replace it with another. When the guys arrive back, I'm not sure who the pee-perp is so I pull the foreman who is quick to lay the blame on his workmate's bladder with the promise it won't happen again. Next morning, once breakfast is over and the guests have left for the day, housekeeping come to me again. Not only have the TWO beds been urinated in, but all of their stuff is gone!

This was taking the piss to a whole new level and suffice to say I was furious!

It was one thing to ruin three mattress's, quite another to then do a runner and leave the bill! Determined not to be outwitted by the weak-bladdered duo I got busy on the phone and put an alert out to the other hotels with a description. I held fire about the bed-wetting, just that they had absconded owing for two nights. No one wants a 'serial-urinater' never mind two, and it was important that I caught them. Something told me that they wouldn't go far and I was right. I received a call at later that day from none other than the hotel I first worked in across the road!

They hadn't long booked in. How did I want to play it? Without delay, I told them I wanted to come over and deal with it myself.

It felt strange walking through that door again and being greeted somewhat differently, because I was an equal now. I was a hotel manager and I had come to collect my debt!

The husband, older but still scary-looking, offered to come up with me. They're in a room right at the top of the house, he said, perhaps I shouldn't go up there alone?

'Oh no,' I had replied demurely, 'I can take care of this by myself, don't worry.'

So it was with the greatest of pleasure when I knocked on their door as they chorused unwittingly *come in!* Their faces, an absolute delight as I went in and cooed 'Hello boys, I've brought you your bill...'

If there's one thing I've learned in all the years I've worked in service, is that wolves in sheep's clothing come in many guises, and my most unsettling guest ever was the suspected murderer.

Now from time to time you'll come across people, who for

whatever reason, life has dealt a bad hand. So you're kindly but not overly so and do what you can do without compromising your professionalism.

One place I managed was such an individual and he would turn up periodically depending on the generosity of the local pastors. I'll call him Daniel, and he was homeless.

Sometimes a minister from the local parish would pay for a night's B&B and Daniel would appear at the door with a shy smile cheque in hand, and I was always happy to accommodate him. He had a quiet manner, some would say odd, and because he was quite insular and never had breakfast I'd stock him up with snacks instead.

Unfailingly polite but I sensed, nevertheless, a surliness beneath the surface and that there was a history best left untapped. But he was never any trouble and always left quietly in the morning.

So it was with great surprise when I received a visit from two police officers one afternoon wanting to know more about my mystery guest.

I asked them why they were making enquiries about him and it soon became apparent that they were reluctant to tell me. The conversation bounced back and fore between us; me, feeling rather protective of Daniel and loath to disclose what little I knew. They, trying to skirt the reason and cautious to the point that in the end I just came right out and said it.

'You think he's the murderer, don't you?'

There had been a local case of some poor woman whose life had been brutally taken – and the suspect was still at large. The caginess of their approach and the kind of questions they were asking didn't need a detective to work it out. The look on their faces told me all I needed to know and I sat back in consternation.

'Daniel?'

They nodded, 'He's just a suspect, mind, and you can't say

anything to anyone. Least of all to him, but he comes here a lot, seems you have a rapport with him, perhaps you can get him to open up.'

I felt my eyes widen in disbelief.

'*Whaaaaat..?* I've had a suspected murderer staying here and you want me to get him to *confess!* Are you serious?' I heard the shrill of indignation in my voice.

'No, no, nothing like that. Just stuff like where he goes when he doesn't sleep here, other guest-houses for instance; usual haunts, you know, that kind of thing.'

I shook my head firmly and laid it on the line.

'You've got to be kidding me! I can hardly get two words out of him as it is, and that's how it works between us. He pays up front, is no trouble, and is given a room. I get a bed filled for the night and one less to cook breakfast for. There is *no way* I'm going to go off-road with this one. He'd smell a rat in no time. No way!'

'You mean he doesn't have breakfast?'

'Nope. Once he's in that room he doesn't come out until the morning, in fact, I wish more guests were like him because he's honestly no trouble. And I'm telling you now, if I start asking him questions he'll get suspicious because that's the kind of guy he is and there's *no way* I'm going to put my life on the line and ask him *anything* other than what flavour crisps he wants!'

I folded my arms across my chest and stared at the police defiantly. It was starting to sink in now that I may have been harbouring a killer for the past few months and I was suitably shaken. I also wasn't prepared to get involved with anything that would put me or my staff at risk.

'Okay, it's okay, we understand, but just keep a close eye on him and call this number should you see or hear anything suspicious.'

I took the card that was offered and said, 'Might be a bit

difficult if I'm *dead!*'

They looked at me askance.

'Well, bloody hell, I've got to look this guy in the eye when he comes by next and all I'm going to hear is the music from 'Psycho' in my head!' I declared, 'How am I supposed to appear normal after *this*!'

'I wouldn't be too concerned, you obviously have a *rapport* with him,' said one of the officers soothingly as though that was the answer to everything, 'so even if he is our man, I doubt he'd hurt you. Just call us if you get worried and make sure to stay on your guard.'

So the next time the bell went and I saw Daniel on the porch, all of my senses went into over-drive. But I forced a smile to my face and greeted him pleasantly as I always did.

An obscure part of me wanted to look deep into those dark eyes, but what would I see? The soul of a man in torment, or something much more sinister? And for that matter did I really want to see anything? I decided not.

Daniel, a killer? Was it possible?

As he followed me down to get his key I took his cheque and loaded him up with his favourite snacks. He didn't seem any different from his usual self, and when he slipped upstairs to his usual room I took a deep breath and tried not to panic. There were other guests in the hotel and good locks on the door to my quarters, I just had to stay cool and try to behave as normally as possible.

I almost wish the police hadn't enlightened me because there are definitely times when ignorance is truly bliss and this was one of them! Now I was beset by a full *frisson* of fear every time I saw him, but I didn't know what else to do.

If I blocked him off completely would my sudden hostility trigger the killer-instinct? And the police were right, I did have a *rapport* with him, but that, I knew from experience could also turn and go the other way.

I was in a Catch 22; damned if I did, damned if I didn't, but the decision was made for me when after several more visits he stopped coming.

I wanted to know why, of course. Had the police got their man? Did he do it? Was he locked up? I called the number they'd given me but they were far from forthcoming and I was left to speculate all manner of possibilities as various scenario's ran through my mind. Perhaps he'd been arrested but they didn't have enough to charge him. Or maybe he knew they were on to him and he'd moved on. It certainly seemed strange that after staying every other week for a year or more he suddenly disappeared into thin air.

I never saw him again or anything in the news, and to this day I often wonder that if he was indeed, a murderer. As I wondered whether it was our connection that kept me off the hit-list or the copious amounts of crisps I gave him thereby sparing myself from a grisly fate. I guess we'll never know, but I've never been able to look at a bag of Smokey Bacon since without a shiver down my spine...

Any role that has a lone woman in a position of authority is often viewed as an easy target. This comes with the territory and when you're the only female sleeping in a house full of men, it also helps to have the ears of a bat. Upon hearing someone prowling outside of my quarters one night saw me pull out my wooden one because there are times when a polite enquiry from behind the door simply will not do. Safely ensconced in my dressing gown I crept towards the door and unlocked it as quietly before throwing it open and leaping out like a Mandingo warrior with a yell fit to wake the dead!

The prowler, turned out to be a rather small man who also happened to be completely naked. At the sight of me brandishing my stick he instantly collapsed to the floor in a parody of worship. The place came alive as other guests stumbled out of their rooms to see what all the fuss was about.

It was as surreal as it was comical as we all just stood there and looked down at the grovelling figure for some moments. He was obviously drunk and when asked what the hell he thought he was doing, he mumbled something about wanting the toilet.

I poked him with my stick. 'What? *On the next floor!'*

He grovelled some more as a few of the regulars offered to evict him, starkers and all into the street. But as tempting as it was, throwing naked guests out of a reputable hotel was not the kind of customer service one should aspire to – as much as it was deserved. But he was threatened with the cellar and sent packing the next morning with his tail between his legs and no breakfast!

Another time as I cruised within a light sleep I was woken by the unmistakable sound of creaky floorboards at the top of the stairs. Someone was doing a runner!

Within seconds I was in my dressing gown and out of the door stick in hand just as two creeping Jesus's were about to open the front door.

'And where do you think *you're* going!'

Their faces were a picture as I glided down the stairs like some outraged Miss Haversham but they had the decency to look ashamed. As they lowered their cases and struggled to make an excuse, it is worth mentioning that they were both mature lecturers who had been visiting for a conference. Hardly the kind of behaviour one would expect from such high-falutin academics, but they coughed up without demur before shuffling past me as I held the door open. Where they went next, I have no idea, but as it was still the early hours of the morning I can only imagine they found a comfortable bench.

I believed I'd seen it all until I met the 'Banner Lady' from the Sally Army. She was small, birdlike, and extremely loquacious. She also had a liking for sherry. Having booked in previously over the phone, she arrived in a high state of excitement with her tasselled flag in tow before entertaining us all in the bar that evening with her exploits.

Now I don't know about you, but when you think Salvation Army and are presented with a tiny elderly lady, you are in some way already conditioned to think they'll behave in a certain way. Well this old dear obviously didn't get out much and this particular trip was the highlight of her year. She'd arrived on the train from somewhere up North to attend a rally, and as a spinster whose life had been devoted to this cause she was really looking forward to it.

As sherry after sherry passed between her lips she became more and more vivacious. After warbling a few hymns she then decided to demonstrate her flexibility. This took the form of executing a series of exercises on the floor that would not have been out of place in the Karma Sutra.

We watched her enrapt! We couldn't believe what we were seeing; to say that she was an eccentric was an understatement and as she rolled about demanding our attention we applauded her performance before the promise of a sherry on the house finally saw her go to bed.

The next morning she tottered into the dining room looking prim and proper in her uniform her banner clutched tightly like an old friend. Despite the many schooners of fortified wine she'd necked the night before she certainly seemed none the worse for wear. Studiously ignoring everyone else she pecked daintily at her plate before checking out with all the dignity of a duchess. Suffice to say she was the topic of conversation for *weeks* afterwards!

It's true to say you have to be open-minded when you work in this kind of business. If a customer wants to talk about the time he saw an alien craft in the back lanes, (and yes, this happened and yes, he swore he saw it!) then prepare to loosen your stays and explore the possibilities. Be amenable when someone wants you to pluck that hair – whether it's from a third eyebrow or dangling from their nose because they're bored and want attention. If you have the tools and the stomach to do it, why not?

But there are limits, however, when you're put in an awkward position via the noble intentions of the misguided do-gooders and the following experience was no exception!

Hearing the bell go one quiet Sunday evening, I answered the door to a well-heeled courteous couple of middle-age who had an air of shiftiness about them that should've warned me.

Did I have a room on the ground floor? They asked

Yes.

Was it available?

Yes.

How much for one night?

I told them and with alacrity the man pulled out his wallet and peeled off some notes.

Delighted with this unusually smooth transaction I invited them in before going to fetch their key as I heard the woman murmur something about going back to the car for something.

Or someone!

Upon my return it was to find them both still stood on the porch and with them the biggest, smelliest tramp I'd ever seen! The sight arrested me for a moment and for a moment I thought I must have been dreaming.

What the hell?

The woman smiled, although a guilty grimace might be a better expression.

'We found him earlier when we came out of church,' she wittered her hands fluttering, 'and well, we wanted to *do* something, you know and so thought it would be a nice to give him a bed for the night...'

She trailed off. I wasn't listening. There were no words.

I looked to her husband who was shuffling his feet looking suitably embarrassed because they knew and *I* knew that I'd been well and truly stitched up!

A silence drew out we all just stood there in an awkward tableau as I inwardly battled to balance their act of Christianity with the fact they had duped me.

What was I to do?

I looked to the recipient of their good intentions and he gazed back at me with all the expectation of a life full of rejection and I couldn't do it.

I stepped back and opened the door wider. There were only a couple of guests in that night, he'd be tucked away downstairs and besides, he was here now, the room had been paid for. It wasn't an ideal situation - what else could I do?

'Come on in, then.'

The tramp was evidently expecting an outright refusal and paused uncertainly.

I jerked my head. 'Come on.'

As he shambled past me I turned to glare at the do-gooding duo but they were already scuttling down the path to their car.

The murder in my heart soon dissipated as I showed my unexpected guest into his room and his obvious pleasure at being in what must have been like opulent surroundings. He dumped his bag and gazed about and I couldn't help but feel sorry for him.

'Are you hungry?'

He nodded.

'Would you like some bacon and egg?'

His eyes lit up.

'Black pudding?'

He beamed.

'Mug of tea?'

His face glowed.

Soon I had him ensconced in an armchair with a tray on his lap, the TV on and instructions how to work the remote. He was pitifully grateful and considering his bulk, his manner bovine-like and gentle. I was still ticked off at the Good Samaritans pulling a fast one but it wasn't his fault. I soon found myself running around after him for want of anything better to do on a Sunday night - and besides, when would he get such an opportunity to be spoilt again!

Later as I helped him off with his shoes, it became apparent why he had needed a room on the ground floor; he had a clubfoot. I held my breath and soon had him all tucked in beneath the duvet a smile of such happiness on his face it made it all worth it.

'Don't forget, if you need the loo, there's one just down the hall.'

He raised a few fingers by way of polite enquiry.

'Yes, what is it? Aren't you warm enough, would you like a blanket?'

'A bucket...'

I looked at him askance.

A bucket?

'Whatever for?'

He gestured apologetically and fixed me with those hang-dog eyes.

'In case I don't make it to the toilet,' he said timidly, 'Sometimes in the night...I... my foot...'

'Yes, of course, I get it.'

And I thought I did. The man was partially disabled with a deformed foot, and waking up in the middle of the night for

a pee could present a problem, so I bustled off to find a
suitable receptacle thinking, how considerate, what a
sweetheart!

I went to bed that night with all the fervour of Mother
Theresa of a job well done and was still aglow with my
medley of good deeds when I got up the next morning.
My air of satisfaction soon dissipated however as I came
downstairs into what I can only describe as a stink!
Without further ado I wedged the front door open before
launching myself into the downstairs room in dread of what
I'd find. *Had he died in the night? Should I have insisted he
at least have had a good scrub before bed?*
My first sight was of the tramp all but cowering beneath the
coverlet and then my eyes and my nose took in the bucket!
Full and stinking to the brim with everything that this man's
bowels had thrown at it and my first thought was *how could
there be so much?*
As the cringing culprit of this bubbling mass mumbled
something about supper being too rich, I held up my hand
and my breath, and went to it as the term 'slopping out'
became a literal reality. But with two guests due for
breakfast I had to work fast and there was no time for
sensibilities.
'Stay there, just *stay there!'* I hissed to the hump beneath the
bedclothes, 'Don't move until I've sorted this out and seen
to the other guests!'
He nodded miserably still trying to make excuses for the
unpredictability of his intestines but I waved them aside. I
wasn't mad at him. The poor sod couldn't help it. But what a
horrible and malodorous start to the day and the clock was
ticking.
Frenetic in my attempts to remove any residual evidence of
the stench saw me rush round like a woman possessed!
Amidst clouds of air-freshener, steams of hot water and

every possible aperture open in the building it was as race against time as I sprayed and cursed, my marigold-clad hands a blur. By the time the two guests had appeared for breakfast, the air was filled only with the smell of bacon but I was in a near state of collapse.

But the show, as they say, must go on, and after I flipped the last egg and the guests checked out, there was renewed murder in my heart for duo who had put me in this position. I went back to the source of my trouble who had got himself up and dressed. He was sat miserably on the end of the bed waiting.

'I'm sorry,'

I sighed. Thankfully there was just the faintest aroma left in the room to indicate what had happened and I was just grateful he'd managed to keep it all in the bucket.

'It's okay, but I think it's best you hit the road, Jack. I've made you some butties you can take with you and some tea in an old flask. That's the best I can do, I'm afraid, it's time to go, my friend.'

Mother Theresa was back. Now that the stress levels had come down from their dizzying heights I was keen to get him out, but not unkindly so. Handing him a carrier bag I led the way to the front door and pulled it open when I suddenly realised he wasn't behind me.

I turned back to find him hovering a few steps back the hang-dog eyes in earnest.

'What is it? Have you forgotten something?'

He gave me what he thought was his best smile before it faded to be replaced by a look of determined hope. What was this? I waited.

'Well?'

The feet gave a little shuffle and he glanced down at them

before raising his eyes back slowly up to my face.

'My refund...'

'*What!*'

I stared at him dumbfounded. *Refund?* I had been expecting all manner of delay-tactics, perhaps even a plea to have use of the bucket for second night - but not this.

'My refund,' he reiterated. His tone had become self-righteous and I felt my jaw flop. Had I missed something?

'A refund...for what?'

We stared at each other; he with all the desperation of someone who has thrown the last card, me with a slow-rising anger. The Amazonian Woman was *not* happy!

'Well, I couldn't sleep, see,' he said in a whiney voice, 'I'm not used to being in a bed so I went outside and slept on the grass instead.'

I was speechless, and pressing forward what he obviously thought was his advantage he added, 'So as I didn't actually spend the night in the bed, see, I came back in early this morning which means I'm entitled to a refund so...'

'*So...what..?*' I intoned dangerously.

The slow-burning anger was unravelling. I didn't have any energy left for a full furnace of temper, but I could feel my whole becoming suffused with the kind of heat usually associated with dragons that have been teased awake and then prodded for good measure.

The 10ft Amazonian began to rise.

Without any kind of conscious effort I could feel myself beginning to expand. Upwards!

It was one thing to have had this unfortunate individual foisted upon me. Another to have then waited on him hand and foot. But to be presented with the entire contents of his bowels before the sun was even up had pushed beyond boundaries even Mother Theresa would've balked at. And now he had the temerity to ask me for a refund!

'Get out!' I barked.

He flinched, his shaggy eyebrows going into some kind of dance.

'Wha...'

'OUT!' I bawled and this time he jumped his belly jiggling.

'But...'

'But *nothing!* Get out before I call the bloody police! I've had *enough!'*

He sidled towards me his whole demeanour a picture of reproach as I glared at him in fury; Mother Theresa had well and truly left the building. He paused, a puzzled look in his eyes and I could almost hear his thought. *Where had the lovely kind landlady gone?*

'Bu...'

I flung out an arm and pointed to the street.

'NOW!'

The people on the bus stop outside couldn't help but hear me roar and now we had an audience goggling over the hedge. Slow-moving traffic slowed even more as the usual Monday morning rush hour became infinitely more interesting as a scene unfolded as a modern-day David tried to evict Goliath. Eventually I won out and he was still whining as he limped off down the path. I remained in place long after he'd gone. Transfixed by the audacity of the man and breathing in fume-filled air that was a welcome change from the more noxious aromas I'd been dealing with.

If any more Good Samaritans came a-calling with cash a-jingling upfront I wouldn't be taken in again. There would be a solemn oath taken on the bible at the very least to ensure no more nasty surprises...

Fortunately there are wonderful, heart-warming encounters that sweeten the memories. Take the Eastern European rugby team who descended in spectacular style! They were booked in for the weekend and as Friday is busy check-out day, we all knew we had our work cut out for a quick turn-round as they were due in just before midday.

Now usual check-in time, as we all know, is after 2pm – at the earliest. But because this particular party would be arriving by coach such timetables don't often take into account the fact we have to service the rooms first. I was amenable to an early arrival on the proviso they only drop off their luggage.

The first sign I have that everything isn't going to go to plan is when I'm cooking breakfast at 6.30 and the phone rings.

'We're parked around the corner. I know we're early, but the team is desperate to get off the coach – can we come in?'

It was the driver and his voice had an edge of desperation to it. Picking up on this and the unmistakable implication therein I felt my eyes go immediately out on stalks.

'No. *No!* I'm in the middle of cooking breakfast, there are people still in bed, no, you *can't* come in yet!'

'How long?' he'd dipped his voice but the desperation was more evident and I knew I'd have to assert myself.

'Half past eight at least, I can't let you in before that. I need to do bills and all sorts. Please, stay where you are until then.'

'Half...past...eight..?' he breathed and with all the disbelief of the condemned man who knows the dreaded moment is here, 'We've been sat here since five... we've been on the coach for three days...I don't know how much longer I can...*hold them...*'

Hold them? *Hold them?*

I felt myself becoming impatient and the Amazonian Woman raised her head. I was also aware that the bacon needed turning and that my waitress hadn't arrived. This was not the time to try and *hold me* to ransom. I waved the spatula in my other hand warningly oblivious to the fact he couldn't see it.

'Yes, yes, I understand but you're just going to have to sit tight a bit longer. Now if you'll excuse me I have other guests to see to, and I'll see you at half past eight!'

I hung up the phone before he burst into tears, or worse, and went about my preparations as the waitress finally rolled in.

I was just flipping an egg for the last customer when I heard a cacophony from the hall that was swiftly followed by a thunderous stampede up the stairs.

It didn't take a rocket scientist to work this one out and I flew out from the kitchen, full breakfast in hand, aghast that this was actually happening. *We were being invaded!*

A tall skinny man was coming towards me all but wringing his hands as he stuttered with apologies, and seeing a long-suffering look in his eyes, I immediately knew he was the driver.

'I'm so sorry, I couldn't stop them, I'm so sorry I couldn't stop them...'

I flashed him a furious look before sweeping past and into the dining room. Thankfully the guests, for the most part were regulars, and they sat, gawping, eyes to the ceiling as the thunder now reverberated throughout the house.

I placed the last breakfast down with all the dignity I could muster, mumbled something about a rugby team and a long coach journey before flying up the stairs to be met by half-naked men running around and complete chaos!

My waitress, to be fair, had deserted her duties in a futile bid to stop them, but they had been like an unstoppable wave; she had no chance.

I, too, soon found myself gawping as two dozen big burly men threw all caution, courtesy and clothes to the wind in their sheer desperation to delve into hot water and wash off the hell of a three-day journey. Not even my private bathroom was spared as bodies, both dry and dripping raced about floors jabbering in their own language.

It was just gone eight o'clock and too much to take in, visually, never mind anything else, and snapping my mouth shut I jerked my head at the waitress and we made our way downstairs in a kind of numbed shock.

The driver was still waiting, and now with an air of dreaded anticipation. After such an unseemly and forbidden entry, I had every right to pull the plug and kick the lot of them out and he knew it. The fact the bill had been paid in advance meant I was (for once) holding all the cards, and he was noticeably cringing as doors slammed and floors shook above us, and sensing his despair, how could I blame him.

'Would you like a cup of tea before you have your shower?' As he practically sagged with relief the waitress and I threw him a mug of tea as we tried to salvage what was left of the morning. The guests, as in the regular guests, were incredibly understanding, and retrieved whatever baggage they had left in their rooms in cheery bemusement.

'See you next week, Mand,' they all chorused with the parting shot, *'if you survive!'*

From what I'd seen so far I doubted it, but once they were all refreshed and showered, cue another stampede as the driver was swept out of the door and on to their respective club.

When the cleaner turned up and saw the state of the rooms she was suitably shell-shocked, and there was nothing for it but to muck in. The waitress was also happy to stay on and help and between us we got stuck in.

'What's this? What are these?' I heard one of the girls call from the room next door.

'What?' I called back in bemusement, since when could I look through walls?

'These...these...long *brown things*...'

I almost went through the wall in my haste to investigate further. Had the mad rush we'd witnessed also involve some belated bowel movements and no mind with which to dispose of them? There were only six toilets in the hotel all told, and with twenty four men having just descended in dire need of deep ablutions, well, once again there's no need for a scientist and I entered the room in dread of what I'd find.

'This!' queried the cleaner and held up a long speckly brown length of *something* that was partially wrapped in paper.

I stopped, then edged closer and stared.

She put it to her nose.

'Don't!' I cried, but it was too late. I held my breath as she gave the brown tip a tentative sniff before turning to me with a confused look.

'It's bread!'

'Bread?'

She nodded. 'Bread.'

I came closer still and took in the sight of rough brown dough.

'Look, there's more of it! It's everywhere!'

And sure enough, in every room, we came across crusts, half-eaten and whole loaves of dry bread. Nothing else, no fruit, or cheese or anything to indicate they had any kind of culinary accompaniment to go with it as realisation dawned. These poor buggers were literally that – *so poor* their only sustenance on the long journey over had been a few loaves of bread a-piece, unless they'd already eaten the good stuff first, of course...

'Shall I bin 'em?'

No, don't you dare! They'll probably still need them. They're only booked in for breakfast with us so I'm assuming the club will be feeding them today, so no, leave them where they are.'

It changed everything and I just couldn't get that bread out of my head.

We didn't see them again until the next morning. After their thunderous and unmitigated arrival the morning before, they had obviously been worded and had crept in like mice and gone quietly to their rooms.

With the waitress who was feeling rather nervous, I went into the dining room to greet them properly and welcome them to the hotel. It was all a bit late, of course, but I was curious about them, these men and their bread. And although they didn't speak a word of English between them they got the message nevertheless and beamed at me happily.

They had been expecting a telling-off, the driver told me, and looking around at the smiley, happy faces I was glad I'd kept my peace. They sat, like obedient children in a classroom as they waited for their breakfast and it suddenly occurred to me that having come from an Eastern Bloc country where life was tough (and full of brown bread), this trip was probably like Las Vegas to them. Without further ado I went into full Mother Theresa mode and thought, *Ah sod it!*

Out came extra sausages, more bacon and lots of WHITE toast as I doubled up on the beans and threw in an extra egg. I knew I'd probably get ii in the neck for such blatant debauchery, but let them have a breakfast they'd remember as they mouthed brown bread on the long journey home. Not everyone who stayed had full English anyway, so what was a bit extra! Just seeing the pleasure on their faces made the prospect of sudden unemployment well worth it.

I did the same the following morning, and every last bit was wolfed down and a pattern barely left on the plate as the driver smiled and nodded. He would have a happier load going out on his bus than he did coming in, and when it was finally time to check out, the team captain indicated he had something for me.

I waited as he rummaged in his bag, thinking, *not bread, no*

*please, not the bread...*because what else did they have?
It soon became apparent.

A can of beer, probably the *last* can of Estonian beer and I
couldn't have been more chuffed! To anyone else, perhaps,
it wasn't much, but to me, having seen how what little they
had and how lightly they travelled, it was massive!

You could keep your last Rolo – this was the epitome of
wanting to give something when you have nothing and I
accepted this precious offering like it was an Elixir of
Youth!

I drank it with suitable reverence a few days later and was
pleasantly surprised – but then anything is better than a stick
of stale bread and it's ever affected my view of the
wholemeal loaf ever since!

It's nice to wind down this chapter on a humorous note,
because despite all the dark souls I met, I also had the
pleasure of meeting some really lovely people and made
many good friends who remain in my life today.

GHOSTLY GUESTS AND STRANGE HAPPENINGS

I've had plenty to say about the living – but what about those who have passed and are no longer with us...or are they?

I've seen and heard enough to convince me, and that's my personal belief. But what makes it more intriguing is when workmates have experienced the same phenomena, and sometimes when you're together...

Old houses, Manor houses, Historic hotels, I've worked in the lot. And yes, I'm aware the very age of some of these buildings can instil an atmosphere and have you jumping at shadows. But I also know that I have witnessed phenomenon that remains unexplained to this day.

So where to begin?

At the social club without a doubt, because not only was I the only recipient of strange happenings - it was also where I saw my first ghost.

I cleaned here in the mornings as well as evening shifts behind the bar. It was a very large Victorian house complete with a cellar, and whilst the clubhouse was a nice, jolly place when other people were around, the atmosphere distinctly became different when you were on your own.

The cellar was bad enough, and some of the staff, including

myself, refused point-blank to go down and change a barrel. The feeling of being watched was so overwhelming you'd all but trip over yourself in the haste to get up those steps and back to the bar.

Many a poor customer was dragged down for protection and to watch out for 'the ghost' as you changed the bitter or grabbed a crate of mixers. Cleaning the place in the morning, however, was a whole different ball-game as things would take on a more 'lively' vibe.

As you polished and cleaned your way through the ground floor bar, noises would start in the one above. This was the bar of the 'shushing' musicians and there was certainly nothing *shush* about it now as whatever was up there began a performance all of its own. It would sound as though furniture was being dragged about (or a body) and you always tried to ignore it because you *knew* there was no one else in the building just as you *knew* you had to go up there next. There is only one other place I've worked where I've had this kind of phenomena happen, and besides being extremely unsettling – although perhaps the term, terrifying, might be more apt – I've since come to the conclusion that *they* who make these noises do so deliberately because *they* want you to know *they* are there!

Bottom bar finished you can delay it no longer, and as another series of bumps shake the ceiling you glance up apprehensively. There is a strong desire to be anywhere else than here right now but you have to finish the job. You *have* to go up there.

So up the stairs you go with that sense of dread usually reserved for the bit in the film when people shout at the poor sap on the screen, *don't go in there!* But that poor sap is you and the bills have to be paid.

With nothing more than a mop for protection and a can of

furniture spray you ascend the stairs slowly.

You can still hear the noises, and the closer you are, yes, it actually sounds as though someone is walking about as well as moving furniture! Yet this can't be possible *because you are the only one here...*

You pause because fear truly has you in its grip, and then you hear a strange wheezing and realise your mouth is wide open and that the shrill whistling you're hearing is your breathing.

Okay, calm down. Come on, just keep going. One foot in front of the other, one foot in front of the other; it becomes almost a mantra. The stairs bring you up to the landing and the door comes into sight. It is closed, as it always is but the sounds beyond carry on unabated.

You come off the last step and on to the landing. The noises are *really* loud now and your eyes are riveted to the door.

You so do not want to go in there but there is no choice so you gird yourself and move forward now hardly daring to breather at all. As you reach the threshold your eyes are wide, every sense is on full alert and then, just as you put your hand out to turn the knob, the sounds stop.

Immediately. Instantly. As though a switch has been flipped, there is sudden and complete silence.

You wait, you listen, your head cocked to the door, but all you can hear is your heart thumping as the blood rushes through your ears.

Nothing.

Slowly, carefully, you push the door open, and still wearing the gaping fish-look you step cautiously inside half-expecting to see *something.*

But there is nothing. As usual the room is empty.

You close your mouth with an audible snap and straighten up, aware that your whole body has adopted a goblin-like hunch poised for flight.

141

The breath you've been holding now comes out in a *whoosh*, you blink with relief and maybe even giggle a little – but the fear is still there.

You dust and polish at a speed people can only dream of as you flick quick glances around the room, especially when your back is turned, and you're really not happy about putting on the hoover because that will then drown out any *sounds* – or anything creeping up on you. Fear is contagious and by this point your mind is running wild.

I can look back now and almost laugh at how I must have looked as I whizzed through the room like some crazy woman, the whipping dusters, the mad look in the eyes as I yanked and threw the hoover about like it was a living thing. It didn't happen every time, but it happened enough to make working there extremely uncomfortable. After several episodes I spoke to the other cleaner who had experienced the same thing and was equally scared. Between us we decided that working under such circumstances was unacceptable and that something had to be done. We presented our case to the Steward who after we'd finished obviously had a hard time keeping a straight face.

But what can I do? What do you expect me to do, girls?' he'd said earnestly, but the twitch at the corner of his mouth belied his concern. He was kindly enough, but then what do you do with something like this? It was also quite obvious that he didn't believe us.

We retreated muttering about working in a haunted house and still adamant that there was something or *someone* about and that we were *not* happy!

The final straw came as we worked together one morning after a particularly busy night and the till went off by itself. We shrieked like a pair of banshees, downed tools and ran next door to where the assistant manager had a flat and roused him from his bed.

Suffice to say he was not amused, but we refused to go back unless he came with us. Grumbling his discontent, he threw some clothes on and sat shaking his head as we flew through the rest of the chores like a desert wind.

I quit the cleaning side after that morning and just stayed with the bar; but whatever was there lurking in that building wasn't done with me yet as I soon discovered several weeks later.

It is said that a ghost, or spirit, will usually appear when you least expect it. That you have to be in a certain state of mind in order to 'see' a manifestation, and I swear on my life that anything ghostly or even remotely spooky was far from my thoughts that night.

It was a Friday and after-hours. A couple of customers had stayed on with staff for a late takeaway supper and a few drinks. It had been an exceptionally busy night, and the food now eaten we were all just chatting and relaxing in one corner of the room.

I was idly listening to the conversation and had looked up, as you do, to the open door behind the bar. It is said that in any given situation, if a door is open in a room your eyes will automatically go to it. Whether this is true or not, or maybe because subconsciously I felt I was being watched, my eyes went to that door and that's when I had the shock of life.

Standing just outside in the hall was the figure of a woman, and she was staring straight at me!

It was as though I received an electric shock, and I'm still not sure to this day if that was some kind of energy I was feeling (emitting?) or as a result of the fear that flashed through me. And I was shocked as much by the look on her face as I was at seeing my first ghost because she was one pissed-off lady!

I could only see the upper half due to the bar, but she was tall, about mid-forties, wearing a high-necked blouse and with two brown plaits coiled on either side of her head.

I can see her clearly now as I did that night. I also recall the sheer hostility in her face; indeed I don't think I'll never forget it. She stared at me with such hatred there was a brief moment when I actually wondered if someone had got locked in, she looked so *real!* But the odd hair-style, the fact I'd never seen her before, not to mention some kind of sixth sense told me emphatically, unequivocally, that yes, I was seeing an actual ghost and I let out a squeal.

'Look! *Look!*' I cried and gestured madly towards the bar, but as soon as I opened my mouth she was gone!

Overcome with emotion my eyes filled up and I was visibly shaking as everyone looked at me in bemusement. Of course no one else had seen the figure and I was teased mercilessly as they sniggered amongst themselves. They all knew about my spook-fest experiences in the place and the fact I wouldn't change a barrel on my own, so this was put down to yet another example of my 'overactive imagination'.

Let 'em, scoff! I thought as my shaking hand reached for a drink, *I know what I saw and whoever this woman is, she's well hacked off we're here, that's for sure. We are in* her *house!*

How I knew this I don't know, but it was as though the look she'd given me had transferred this information and I knew in my heart it was true. Small wonder there had been noises and disturbances. She'd probably been all but breaking her spiritual neck trying to make her presence known in the hope of scaring us out!

But it was the look on her face that has always stayed with me, and it was a look I knew well. When I was growing up I had a friend I would call on whose mother often behaved oddly. Your reception would depend on her mood. One day she would be all smiles and bid you enter. The next she would fix you with a nasty stare before slamming the door in your face. As a child you kind of accepted these things, but I've never forgotten that stare or the naked hostility within it. It was the look that said *Go away* only in this instance more of a *Get out!* Perhaps she picked me to show herself because she knew *I knew* there was someone/something there. It wasn't a friendly visit and far from a pleasant experience and I've never seen the like again. But I've seen other things though and I've *heard*. Oh yes, I've heard plenty...

But firstly let me tell you about an odd experience whereby the resident ghost was actually very friendly. Indeed I'd even go as far as to say helpful, and with a liking for showmanship.

And so take, if you will, another cellar in another large house built in an era when horses drew carriages and tumble dryers were yet to be invented.

There you'd find the usual stuff that was integral to running a hotel; cleaning products, spare bedding, camp beds, a washing machine and the aforementioned dryer. It was also where the safe was kept so the door was kept locked at all times and only I had access to the key.

Like anyone running a business solo there are times when you leave certain things meaning to do them later, and in this instance I was always guilty of allowing the empty detergent containers to build up upon and around the machines. So imagine my surprise when I went down one morning only to find a neatly-stacked pyramid of empty containers sat proudly atop of the dryer!

I think my jaw hit the ground, never mind my chest and I ran back up the stairs hollering for the waitress to come and take a look!

One of our regular guests was still about so I also insisted
that he, too, come down to the cellar and bear witness to this
incredible sight.

Both were suitably spooked as they were impressed and we
stood marvelling at the strangeness of how this could have
occurred – and seemingly overnight. You had to pass the
machines to get to the safe and having deposited that day's
takings as I always did at the end of the night, there was
certainly no empty receptacle pyramid there then!

It's a shame that we didn't have mobile phones in those days
like we do now as it would've been great to have had a
picture for posterity. But one thing was for sure, whoever, or
whatever had created that stack was trying to tell me one of
two things; either someone was around and wanted to make
their presence known – or for me to stop being such a lazy
mare and take my rubbish out!

With a sense of almost reverent awe I dismantled the
pyramid and scattered the containers in the hope it would
happen again. And it did, a few days later and I was cock-a-
hoop! It was my way of ascertaining that this phenomenon
had actually occurred, but it never happened again and I
took a strange comfort that there was something benign in
the house that simply wanted me to know it was there
without scaring me.

Some spirits, however, are not so accommodating, and will
go out of their way to give you the heebie-jeebies. Take the
place with the turn-downs for instance. Large, rambling,
with centuries of history and so much activity it had its own
Ghost-book! Now I know you'll all remember the drill with
this particular aspect of pretentious hospitality, and so there
I am one night showing the ropes to a newbie. She hasn't
done turn-downs before so the process is slower than usual.

By the time we come to the final room it's starting to get dark and the wind has picked up adding to the whole 'Hotel Hammer House of Horror' vibe.

I knock at the door, pause for a few moments, and then knock again reminding her as I'm doing it that we always knock twice – just in case.

Hearing nothing, I put the key in the lock, turn it and just as I'm opening the door there comes from the darkness a snarling voice. *Whoops!* Looks as though we've disturbed someone and they're far from happy about it!

'Sorry, *sorry!*' I call out and I'm absolutely mortified.

Not only have I committed a *coup de grace* in front of a new staff member, but we've just disturbed a guest who was seemingly fast asleep. No doubt there would be a complaint going in, but in my defence, I did give the two required knocks.

Feeling rather embarrassed and knowing I'd have to 'fess up, I led the way down to the bar behind which was one of the owners was acting Maitre'd that night. I was all but shuffling my feet as I told her all the rooms were done except for Room 12. They were sleeping – or at least they had been until I'd woken them up but there was no *Do not Disturb* sign outside the door and the newbie would confirm I gave the requisite two knocks.

I lifted my eyes to my boss's face expecting to see the usual frosty disapproval but there was puzzlement instead.

She gave me a long look before nodding her head towards a couple in the corner.

 'They can't be. Room 12 are right over there.'

It was one of those moments when there should've been a burst of dramatic music you have in the films when it becomes clear that there *is* something in the attic, or in the cellar, or in the *room*, and as my boss and I stared at each other I heard the new girl gasp.

'No,' I said gathering myself with a small laugh, 'there *was* someone in the room.' I turned to my fellow witness.

'Wasn't there? *We heard them!*'

She nodded her eyes huge in her face.

My boss drew herself up and assumed a haughty expression, 'Well I'm telling you now, Room 12 are sat right over there and have been for the past thirty minutes.' Her expression flickered as she murmured as an afterthought, 'So... another one for the ghost book, then.'

The new girl squeaked, 'What ghost book?' She had a look about her much like a deer on the brink of flight and I felt my heart drop.

It was difficult to find staff that could drive, and this place was so far out in the sticks I was keen not to lose her.

I tinkled another laugh and tried to play the whole episode down.

'Oh it's nothing. It was probably just the wind. Come on!'

As I turned away there came another squeak. I turned back.

'What is it?'

The squeaker gulped and stuttered trying to find the right words as I gave her what I hoped was a reassuring look.

'Come along, we still have to turn the room down and the sooner it's done the sooner we can go home!' I forced a cheeriness I didn't feel into my voice and led the way.

'What! *What?* We're going back up *there?* '

'Yes, my love, I'm afraid we're going to have to. Look, don't worry, it probably was just the wind it's been a long day, we're both tired and your ears can play tricks when you...'

I broke off in the realisation I was suddenly addressing thin air.

The new girl had stopped and was gazing at me shaking her head slowly.

'That wasn't the wind and you know it. We *both* know it.

The wind doesn't make sounds like *that!*'

I sighed. She was right, of course. Indeed the wind couldn't have made the unintelligible but unmistakable sound of someone being roused from sleep. It was the kind of noise you hear coming out of the mouth of an angry drunk.

Initially I'd assumed that the guest wasn't feeling very well and had taken to their bed for an early night, or perhaps they had enjoyed an afternoon session and were simply sleeping it off.

Two things were certain, however; whoever had made that sound had done it deliberately, and secondly, we had to go back in to that room.

I dropped the jolly tone and lowered my voice, 'Okay, I'll come straight. This is a very old house. It's been here hundreds of years and sometimes things happen we can't explain, and whatever it was in Room 12 - let's just say that it was a grumpy ghost with an odd sense of humour. He or it, can't hurt you, or do anything more than make nasty noises. So come on, let's show him we're not frightened, eh?'

'But *I am* frightened!'

I gazed at her with a mixture of appeal and pity and she capitulated, albeit reluctantly. With dragging steps she followed me back up to Room 12.

This time I didn't knock. I was weary after a long day but keen to show confidence and I unlocked the door with a flourish before marching in.

It was practically pitch black inside as the curtains had already been drawn by the occupants and without further ado I switched on the lamps and made my way to the – empty – and still neatly-made bed. The new girl followed me cautiously her eyes everywhere as though expecting something to jump out at her. The wind moaned as we went about our duties in silence and I felt her fear and just knew she wouldn't be back.

A phone call into the office the next morning confirmed her cessation of employment with immediate effect; and her reason? The place was simply too scary for her.

Ironically the rumbling revenant in Room 12 wasn't the only one who liked to make itself known. Across from the main building was the old stable block that had been converted into two large suites, and it was in the upper one where it would seem there resided a more permanent guest.

As you went about your business during the day there was nothing more sinister than a strong sense of being watched, but when the night-time came – it was a whole different kettle of fish.

As you made your way across the cobbled yard your eyes would be on the windows wondering if 'they' or 'it' were watching you approach. You always had that sense that they were waiting for you. But it wasn't until you were in and servicing the suite below that the noises would start and then, you'd have to gird yourself.

I believe I mentioned earlier that I'm a bit of a stomper, well let me tell you that I'm a positive ballerina in comparison to the stamping that went on up there.

Deliberately.

Oh yeah, I never had any doubt of that...

All of the girls who had done turn-downs had heard it and it appeared to particularly like performing for the housekeeping staff. My feeling was that whatever it was, its aim was not just to frighten, but to deter you completely from going up those stairs.

I'd be lying if I said I wasn't disturbed by this. It was scary but it was also intriguing in a funny kind of way, and it didn't happen all the time, just regularly enough to keep you on your toes. The intense feeling of being watched, however, never abated and whatever it was it definitely wasn't friendly, that's for sure!

My way of dealing with it was to adopt a no-nonsense tone and tell it off! How else was I ever going to open that door at the bottom of the stairs in the knowledge there was something up there waiting? And it helped. The noises would stop as soon as you put the key in the lock and the sudden silence that followed was as unnerving as was the sound of the heavy stomping.

Exactly the same phenomena as I'd experienced in the Social club but I was more confident now and besides, I had the 10ft Amazonian Woman.

'Don't bloody start now!' I'd say loudly as I made my way up the stairs, 'I've had a long day and I'm bloody knackered. Just don't start your games with me now, *please!'*

No reply would be forthcoming, of course, but there was always that intense awareness within the room and the hair would prickle at the back of your neck. In a bid to retain your nerve you'd find yourself babbling about anything and everything for as long as it took to get the job done. Sometimes as soon as you finished and shut the door the noises would start up almost immediately. But you were never tempted to go back up and investigate. Same as when you made your way across the yard and you'd feel unseen eyes on your back - you never turned around to look, because sometimes it's simply best not know...

These instances of inexplicable phenomenon were for me most compelling. Yet the most memorable experience was when I was hotel-sitting and woke up one night to the sound of snoring in the bed next to me!

Like the previous establishment with the stomping ghost, this too, was an extremely old Welsh manor house that was reputedly haunted. Although much smaller than its counterpart, it had, nevertheless, that same air of watchfulness about it with the feeling that you were intruding in some way.

I was the general assistant and when the owners were called away on urgent family business, I had the task of not only deputising for the week, but also keeping an eye on their two children. As they were both teenagers they were self-sufficient enough to warrant nothing more than cooking their tea.

As I would be staying over for the duration I took a room near the old servant stairs above which the family had their quarters. The idea was I would be close should either of the children suddenly call out in the night and with this in mind I would leave my door ajar.

In view of the hotel's reputation for having more than one ghost, it was not a decision I took lightly, but my apprehension was superseded by my sense of duty and I prepared myself for any bumps or strange noises in the night.

It is worth mentioning that there were areas in that place where you felt distinctly uncomfortable as though you were trespassing in some way. In fact I have never before or since stayed worked in such an unfriendly house. Not even the Hammer Hotel of Horror with the turn-downs was as bad and that was saying something!

There was a lovely chaise-longue in the main lobby that sat before a beautiful fireplace. One night, as there were no guests in I decided to treat myself and light a fire with visions of reclining in comfort with a glass of wine and my book.

Unfortunately I only lasted a few minutes because the feeling of hostility became so overwhelming I put the guard up and crept back to the kitchen which was the only part of the house that felt 'okay'.

With this in mind, and aware that my sense of these things was acute, I had deliberately closed myself off which made the shock all the more terrifying when I woke up to find I was no longer by myself in the bed!

I can almost picture it now, how my eyes flew open and stared into the darkness as the sound of snoring came from beside me, and it's fair to say that I froze.

It truly is the kind of thing you hope never to hear (whether from the dead or the living!) when you've gone to bed alone and woken up to find you've got company. But it was happening and I didn't know who or what it was. Somehow I had to snap out of the paralysis and *put the bloody light on!* The snoring was coming from my left, so I reached out slowly for the lamp switch to my right, and despite dreading what I would see, I kept my eyes firmly in the direction of the sound as my fingers found the switch and then...
My eyes widened even further as I took in the sight.
I had been expecting an old man, a ghostly knight perhaps, or even a decrepit old servant who had once worked in the manor, and for some moments my brain just couldn't compute what my eyes were seeing.
It was the dog! It was the great big lump of the hotel dog sprawled out next to me like the Queen of Sheba!
The light had woken my canine companion and she opened one eye and looked at me happily before giving a snort and going back to sleep. I stared dumbfounded before starting to giggle. I think it was the shock. The dog soon woke up with that and I swiftly evicted her on the promise of some extra treats the next day for *not* being a ghost!
It was such a bizarre experience that in hindsight I often wondered what I'd have done if my bedfellow that night *had* been a ghost – which then raises the question; do spirits sleep? Think you'll have to find the answer to that but suffice to say I slept the remainder of that week with the door shut!

A rather poignant ending to this particular section was a strange occurrence, of which I still have the evidence that happened, the first Christmas after my father had passed away. At the time I was living in and running a hotel in between running back and fore to the hospital as cancer ravaged my father and we waited for the inevitable. Thankfully it came in early December and I was present when he took his last breath. Amidst the grief, the sense of relief was huge; I was practically dead on my feet myself from long hours keeping the business going in between bedside vigils. Knowing my father was finally free from pain also made the aftermath more bearable.

After everyone had checked out on Christmas Eve, I locked down the hotel very much looking forward to a couple of days off and some time to myself. But when I woke up on Christmas morning it was to a most incredible and inexplicable surprise!

Downstairs in the reception area there was a mod-con set-up for the telephone system that recorded & printed every call in or out. It was like a Miss Moneypenny version of a telephone typewriter and had seen many an opportunist cringe before coughing up as the evidence was flourished before them.

Yet despite the fact every room had been empty, except for mine – the printer had been busy during the night. Very busy!

I was met with rolls and rolls of print-out, and what was even more disturbing was that the printer had been operating at such a rate of knots, it had, for want of a better word, burned itself out and become jammed.

I stepped towards it. I had never known it do this before, and I was suitably perplexed. I reached out and pulled the reams towards me wondering what I would find. What had it printed – and more pressing (pun intended) *from which part of the hotel!*

I had been alone. All night. Just me and my cat; but seemingly not...

I looked at the print-out and frowned.

There before me, line after line, row after row, sheet after sheet were *asterisks!* Nothing more, nothing less, just * after * after **

I stared at them and then went to the first part of the sheet to see what time this unprecedented event had kicked off.

Not long after midnight.

I had been fast asleep, yet despite my room being directly above the reception area and the print system not known for being a particularly quiet – I hadn't heard a thing!

What made it more interesting was that the action had also been coming from that particular line and not from another

room – which was some small comfort, I guess!
I carefully unjammed the paper hoping that the intensity of
that final feed hadn't damaged the equipment, and was
surprised to feel that the blackened seam was *still warm!*
I was intrigued more than frightened and couldn't take my
eyes off those asterisks. Even as I sat with my coffee, my cat
on my lap, the asterisks spread out before me like some
bizarre secret code, a thought suddenly occurred to me and I
felt the hairs rise on the back of my neck.

Kisses! The symbols looked like *kisses!* Could it be my
father sending me some Christmas cheer via the telephone
system? Or was the idea completely preposterous? Stranger
things had been known to happen when loved ones reached
out across the divide, and wasn't interference of electrical
appliances one of the most common means of trying to
instigate communication?
My intrigue was now replaced with a deep sense of pleasure
and I gave a small smile. The jury was still out but the
prospect of having possibly received a Christmas card from
the other side with the most kisses *ever,* was as comforting
as it was crazy, yet it wasn't over yet!
This unprecedented activity had literally put a spanner in the
works. I wasn't too unhappy about that; hotel life is ruled by
the phone but it needed to be sorted before the first batch of
guests came in for New Year.
On Boxing Day I managed to find an engineer willing to
come and take a look and I led the way down to the
basement. As he shone his torch into the medley of wires he
gave a low whistle.
'Wow, well you've certainly been busy?'
I looked at him askance.
'What do you mean?'
'Well,' he said, 'you've obviously had a full house with
everyone busy on the phones to have caused this kind of
surge! But then again, I suppose it being Christmas an' all...'
He trailed off as he saw the look on my face.
'I haven't had a full house,' my voice was steady and with
my next words it was his turn to look puzzled, 'There's been

only me here. The hotel closes over Christmas.'
He stared at me and I detected an air of sympathy because he
knew as well as I did the implications of this statement and
it floated between us like an unasked question.
'Can you fix it?' I asked interjecting a bit of realism into
what was turning into a surreal situation.
'Yes, yes, I can fix it,' he replied, and then added hesitantly,
'Are you alright...er...what I mean to say is, are you going to
be...alright?
I knew what he meant, of course and smiled reassuringly.
'Yes, absolutely, I'll be fine.'
As I left him to it and went back upstairs and was assailed
by a warm kind of glow.
Dad? Could it have been you? Was it you? So determined to
reach out and give me a sign you all but blew the gasket! It
was a happy thought and again I found myself smiling.
The Jury had duly returned to their places and the vote was
unanimous.
I almost felt sorry for the engineer when he'd finished and
presented me with the paperwork. It was obvious he was not
happy and not a little spooked.
'Are you sure you're going to be alright here on your own?'
His worried manner was touching. Dusk was setting in and
so was the house as it creaked and groaned as it settled its
three-storeys for the night. Hotels are naturally eerie when
devoid of people and this particular Victorian pile was no
exception.
I gave him a knowing look with an added little twinkle. No,
I wasn't at all concerned. With some of the frights I've had
to deal with coming through these doors, extended Christmas
greetings from my dearly-departed was the least of my
worries!
The phones were sorted. I had one more night of much-
needed peace and quiet with the added comfort of knowing
that somewhere, close by, my father was keeping vigil and
so why would I not be alright?
His face was a picture; he didn't know what to say so he just
nodded and I've never forgotten his kindness. Nor have I the
irony of finally finding a knight who was less concerned

about the living than he was about the dead! But it was an interesting experience, nevertheless and one that suggests to me, at least, that the Ghosts of Christmas *do* exist and not just in 'A Christmas Carol'...

MISCELLANEOUS MOMENTS OF MADNESS

For anyone who has worked in modern-day service life can be exciting, insightful and eventful – but it can also be mind-numbingly boring. Whenever I have found myself in extreme situations of *ennui* it helped to pretend that I was actually an old-style servant when choices were few and opportunities fewer still.

And it's easy to do so when you're sat on an upturned bucket peeling sacks of potatoes in some dingy back room as you question the Universe and your existence in it. There is something soul-destroying about being presented with a mountain of veg, and all you have is a poxy little peeler and hours stretched out before you like an imagined state of purgatory.

Cue the start of a day that could've changed my life. We've all had opportunities, but this was a rare one that began with that sack of spuds in a back room. It was a casual number, just a few days grind in a very large venue where a world-famous band was playing. Local labour had been drafted in and I got lucky courtesy of friends and the lure of some very good pay.

The hours were long, 12 hour days and very few breaks as the catering team whose job it was to keep over 500 fed sped into action like a well-oiled machine. As a friend and I toiled in the semi-darkness we consoled ourselves that it could always be worse, we could be peeling sprouts and besides, just think of the money and the things we could buy.

After a day or two the dishwashing duo quit and we were promoted to 'the sink'. I was very happy about that because you were in the hub of things and could see what was going on. I was happy to wash as my friend was to dry, and we got stuck in as the daily task of feeding the 500 got underway. Every meal was buffet-style and there was lots of it. No sooner had we finished the breakfast debris then the lunch stuff came piling in and so on.

It was akin to being on a treadmill of an endless tea party as the chef and his team worked at full speed and your world shrank into that sink and the constant flow of crockery traffic.

Seeing our loyal application to the task in hand, and the fact we got on very well with the rest of the team, my friend and I were promoted again as the spud girls took over the dishes and some poor saps took on spud-duty.

We couldn't have been more delighted for we were promoted to food prep, no less, which meant no more rubber gloves and more chance to nibble.

Break-times were irregular, you would literally just grab a plate of food and wolf it down because the pace was relentless and the feeding frenzy never stopped. But you had a free-view of the concert if you wanted it and surplus food always came home with you at the end of the night. And always, always, what kept you going was the thought of the money. Talking of which, the woman in charge was never without her bulging bum bag full of lolly, and you couldn't help but allow your jaw to drop as she'd unzip and peel a few notes from a huge wad to give some runner or as payment for goods.

She was streetwise and savvy but she ran a tight ship and for some reason took a liking to us and offered us both a place for the rest of the tour! Top dosh, all flights paid and a chance to travel with a world-class band!

The next stop would be Newcastle then on to Hungary before taking in the rest of Europe. My friend and I were completely blown away – not just by the offer, but that our humble efforts were so obviously appreciated enough to warrant a once in a life-time opportunity.

I often wondered if my life may have turned out differently if I'd gone along on that trip. But I had pets and commitments, and as much as I would have loved the adventure, sadly it was not to be.

Another instance that gave me a peek into the world of the rich and famous was when I worked as castle custodian for a season. For the most part it could be mind-numbingly boring. The only parts I really relished were walking the site at the beginning and end of each day. You'd really get a feel for the place and I enjoyed these lone excursions immensely. So when we got a call one day from the local police their proposal had us all in a flutter. They were staging an exam for two trainee security agents and wanted to use our venue as a part of the exercise. They planned to use a bogus celebrity and needed someone to give them a personal tour as they went through their protection paces in readiness for an equally bogus attack.

It was all very exciting and I was lucky enough to be put forward for this task. I had visions of some kick-ass action in the lower bailey, or perhaps a full-on scrap in one of the towers. I could hardly wait!

On the appointed day a well-dressed and rather flamboyant figure arrived with two dark-suited men in tow wearing the requisite dark glasses and I eased smoothly into my part. I knew, of course, that the VIP was a phoney, but the two guys charged with keeping him safe didn't, and inwardly I was abuzz with the intrigue!

As I guided 'our man' around the castle I found myself scanning for potential assailants almost as keenly as the security guards, and had to make a conscious effort not to keep whipping my head around every time someone appeared.

Not even the two trainees were aware that an attack was going to take place, so I had to keep reminding myself that this wasn't really real and that there was no need for the 10ft Amazonian woman and to just chill.

Our group, too, were beginning to draw quite a bit of
attention as we wandered around the site like extra's from
'The Men in Black'. Some visitors even stopped to gawp,
probably wondering who the VIP was and at times I found it
hard to keep a straight face. Then all too soon the tour was
over and yet nothing had happened! After thanking me
profusely and shaking my hand the VIP and his minders
melted away and I turned to my colleague with a puzzled
frown saying, 'Did I miss something?'
The mystery was solved, however, a few days later when we
received a call from the police to say thank you and I simply
had to ask.
'What happened to the attack when the guys were supposed
to spring into action?'
'Ah, I'm afraid that took place at another location. Yours
wasn't the only one we used for the exercise, you see.'
'Oh.' The disappointment was evident in my voice and I felt
cheated. I had been deprived of my 'James Bond' moment,
all that trotting about and blathering on about medieval
mayhem, and for what? But then that is the notion when
you're in service; you are at the beck and call, the whine and
the whim, the call and command of whoever pays the coin. It
is not for us, the modern day servant to question why – you
are required, simply, to just get on with it.
I have to say at this point that being the custodian of an
ancient monument all sounds rather grand and yet it was one
of the most boring jobs I have ever done. Taking endless
admission payments, citing the standard spiel of castle
history, giving directions to the public toilets and dealing
with unruly and rude coach-loads of school children who had
never heard of the word 'please' often saw me cast my eyes
to heaven as I muttered under my breath.
So when I had to deal with a bunch of drunken Morris Men
who had missed their slot on account of their foray into one
of the local pubs, I all but leapt at the chance for some lively
discourse and let's just say that the lower bailey hadn't seen
such action since the Civil War!
Taking to task two day-trippers who nearly became stuck up
a chimney was also a defining moment, as was the many

would-be ghost hunters and 'adventurers' who would hide at
the top of a tower in the hope of getting locked in. Even now
I can recall the shame-faced shuffle as I escorted them out of
the doors my mouth twitching as I tried not to laugh. But
such exploits didn't happen often enough to keep my interest
and I left just after one season

I've had the pleasure of having done just about every job
there is in the service industry including several care jobs
back in the 80's. But due to the sensitivity of that particular
area I will not touch on my experiences other than to say it
was challenging at times but very rewarding.
I will mention, however that I once had the honour of caring
for a lovely old gentleman who had been in the cavalry in
the Hungarian army – during the First World War! I will
never forget his humble spirit and his enduring love of
horses. I loved to hear the old stories and some of the people
I looked after had lived incredibly interesting lives. Such
work demands the highest calibre of compassion and it was
also a pleasure to work alongside the precious few for whom
it was more than just earning a living.
Unfortunately a back injury made any further forays into this
line of work impossible, as bed-hoists were not
commonplace during those days, and if you couldn't lift then
basically you were useless.
But I did do a brief stint for a lovely aristocratic old lady
some years ago when I was employed as a companion. It was
an interesting and insightful position, and it is my belief I
got the job because I was new to the area and didn't know
the family. For obvious reasons I won't divulge their
identity; again, trust is everything, but I have the most
marvellous memories of a generous-hearted lady who would
embellish our time with the most amazing stories of an era
lost forever, and it would be fair to say she had lived a
wonderful and intriguing life.
But returning to the time of the yuppies, the big hair and the
shoulder-pads. My knackered back saw me return to the
world of hospitality, and it was also around this time when
landed a job working for an old boss.

Remember the Cocktail King in my first waitressing job? He of the loud shirts and gleeful attentions to the Liz Taylor look-a-like? Well he didn't look so gleeful when our paths next crossed as he laboured behind a butchers counter with his wife in charge and cracking the whip!

I marvelled at the change in him and how far the mighty can fall. I also wondered if he would remember me, but as my eyes slid up to his during the interview there wasn't so much as a flicker of recognition. Just the weary look of a man dreaming of better days and I breathed easy.

There was a deli and sandwich section in their shop, and it was my job to make the rolls and baguettes for the hordes of school-children that would descend for their lunch. They were extremely good business and yet another insight into how the other half live.

Having been raised on school dinners and the odd packed lunch, seeing these kids throw their money around for roast beef and mustard, prawns and best ham, I was, in the early days quite in awe. But then this was an affluent part of the city where posh was the norm – but it sure was an eye-opener, especially as the children were always unfailingly polite and showed more respect than most adults.

Sometimes I would secretly watch my old boss as he served and bantered in a half-hearted way with the punters. Such a pale shadow of his former self, the only bright colours he wore was the blood on his whites and I actually felt quite sorry for him. Imagine Shrek being put in a pinny and told to bake cakes and you get the picture.

The worst job for me has to be, without doubt, my time in an industrial laundry. One of the noisiest, dirtiest, dustiest and most soul-destroying jobs I've done (besides cleaning loos) and I lasted just four weeks.

It was pretty much how it must've been back in the old days of the Industrial Revolution when great mills and factories sprang up all over the towns and cities, and poor schmucks like me were pulled in to graft doing the same job hour after hour, day after day, as great machines boomed all around you and the foreman wearing a permanent frown would patrol as he watched you like a hawk.

But he needn't have worried, there was no chance of slacking; such were the noise levels you couldn't even talk to the person next to you without shouting and ruining your throat.

My job was to fold the endless piles of work overalls that were kept in great wicker baskets and such was the grime – even after cleaning – that all the skin on your hands became engrained and you'd have killed for some gloves and some Vaseline!

Such were the stress-levels that when the bell sounded for lunch a few of us would hot-foot it down to the local pub and swig a quick pint before hot-footing it back before the 30 minutes was up. Considering it was a 10 minute stride to the nearest pub, there and back, it gives you some idea of why the poor working classes back in the day turned to gin!

Retail was another nightmare – for the fact it was so boring. Standing around in a shop is not my idea of fun and that too, lasted a short while as I simply slipped away one day mumbling something about having a life. It didn't help that my boss was a stick in the mud in this one particular place. What made it all the more bizarre was that she was younger than me but the rest of the crew were good fun and that always helped. The place was a snazzy Sports shop in the centre of town and was great during the summer whilst the kids were off school. Having been quite athletic back in the day and I enjoyed the job until autumn came and then it all went quiet. Mind-numbingly so.

I would stand in the doorway looking out on the street bored to tears and yearn for something to happen. Well, I got my wish one day when two former work colleagues saw me and came over for a chat. We hadn't seen each other for ages. They were going for a pint across the road – could I take a break and join them? It was just after midday and I'd already had my break. I was down for one o'clock lunch but asked my boss if I could swap with another member of staff.

The answer was a terse no. Not even the cajoling of my ex-workmates would make her change her mind so they took matters into their own hands and kidnapped me there and there on the spot!

Well, I'd been waiting for some form of diversion and it didn't come any better than this! As I was scooped up like a roll of carpet and borne aloft, my boss stuttered in outrage as I giggled uncontrollably. Shoppers stopped to gawp but no one saw fit to intervene of course. Not only were these guys big and on the muscular size, but my laughter denoted quite clearly that I was a willing victim.

As they bore me away to the pub I felt like Cleopatra, and not even the sight of my boss left fuming in the doorway was enough to spoil the moment. It was absolutely hilarious and well worth the rollicking I got afterwards but I soon got another job.

You could in those days. CV's were unheard of, references could be forged, and work was everywhere if you knew where to look.

I'd been a dog-walker, briefly ran a cattery until the owner expanded the job spec and tried to include her two horses and the housework. I've tried my hand at hair-dressing (and lasted one day) worked on building sites, done landscape gardening, and once worked, unforgettably, as an award-winning corporate clown!

What all of my experiences taught me is that there are some great people out there who value their workforce – and sadly there are those who do not.

There tends to be a view that those who work in Hospitality are in some way inferior and worthy of scant respect. And I can tell you almost to the day when a customer pushed me too far and the joy of being of service went cleanly out the window – as did nearly the offending customer!

It's ironic that it should have been one of the 'fairer sex' who pushed the final button. I've had men in my face, been yelled at and insulted, threatened with all manner of violent demise, had a glass put to my face and sexually assaulted – but when it came to it, it was the crass behaviour of one stupid woman that pulled the plug and I never worked in hospitality again.

At that time I'd gone to help out a newly-refurbished

business that the owners had spent heaps on with dreams of running their own pub. Unfortunately, many of the locals, however, had a different idea and enjoyed nothing better than baiting the new proprietors and generally being obnoxious. Add to the mix a staff-force who were blatantly abusive and you had, it would be fair to say, a pretty bad situation.

So when I was approached by the owners with a desperate plea for help, I rose to the challenge immediately. I often look back on this particular part of my career at what I call 'My Roadhouse' (clue is a 1989 film starring Patrick Swayze – although I was distinctly lacking any martial art skills and the pub didn't have strippers), but it did have a drug problem and a nucleus of bully-boys who thought they ruled the roost.

There was only one way to do this and I went at it with gusto leaving a trail of dodgy staff and emasculated men in my wake. The 10ft Amazonian woman well and truly came into her own!

But when you're required to go out amidst a crowd of drunken men, adding an extra inch or two on your shoe doesn't cut it, so I was 'up' more than I was 'down' as I projected my giantess with all the power of an excocet missile!

Projection is a wonderful thing but you have to *believe*. You have to project what is basically is a psychological illusion with all your heart and soul or else it doesn't happen. Psychology is a mighty weapon and fear never comes into it because you get to set the parameters and trust me when I say it *works!*

So when I would leave the safety of a bar and step out to face down the pack, I would rise and rise until I towered above them all before moving purposely into their midst like a Titian amongst men. And as the ground would shake with my imaginary stomp, my face would be set and the 'wolves' would scatter, suddenly unsure. Because there is something *different* about you but they can't put their finger on it, indeed their eyes are telling them one thing and yet some hidden sense quite another. It is this uncertainty that stays their hand because on some obscure and infallible level they *know!*

There would be no confrontation, they would simply melt away and let me through. After collecting empty glasses I would return to the bar with nothing more than confused eyes on my back and an air of suppressed resentment because as much as some of them wanted to have a pop, they weren't prepared to risk it - and certainly not in front of the pack!

I always enjoyed my Amazonian moments and eventually as things started to calm down I could relax a little, especially when the weekends came around.

The drug-dealers had been sent packing, the bully-boys de-beefed, and the staff overhaul meant a smoother and more productive ship.

So I was feeling particularly good one Saturday when I greeted a woman who had arrived early for a dinner reservation. As I smiled and took her coat, little did I she was about to have an impact on the rest of my hospitality career.

There was a nice seating area near the restaurant and I settled her in to wait for her three friends and went off to get the wine list.

Now some people like to make a big thing about wine and you just have to stop your eyeballs rolling as a decision is made with all the drama of a world-shaking event, and this lady was no exception.

She hummed and she hawed, had me back and fore with at least half a dozen bottles until she finally made her choice and I asked if she wanted me to bring four glasses.

'No, just the one will be fine.'

I poured the wine for her to taste. She nodded her approval and I topped up her glass, then, just as I was turning away she called me back.

Can you bring me another glass, please?'

It was starting to get busy, more diners were arriving and already she had taken up more of my time that was necessary. As Front of House it was my job to meet and greet and already there were people wandering about aimlessly. I cast about for a waitress as I suppressed my irritation.

'Yes, of course. Please just give me one moment.' I kept my voice polite but inwardly I wondered what she was playing at.

It soon became apparent, however, when on my return she smiled at me sweetly before saying, 'Oh go on, then. I may as well have another one.'

I looked at her in puzzlement.

'I'm sorry...another what?'

'Another glass...'

Then she looked me right in the eye and *smirked.*

She smirked!

They say that there is a defining moment, an epiphany, an awakening of some kind that comes to us all – and for me this was it.

I was bending down at the time and as I raised my eyes slowly to her face I felt something deep inside me go.

Not in a big or even particularly earth-shattering way, but it was an indefinable shift and I felt my whole face change as I straightened up before this stupid woman and she drew back uncertainly.

For not only was *I* no longer smiling, but I was aware of a sudden darkness in my stare that had nothing to do with smudged mascara and everything to do with serial killers and acts of violence.

'Oh, oh, I'm sorry' she fluttered nervously, because she *knew* in that instant that a button had been pushed. A step had been taken. A boundary had been breached and that if I'd had a custard pie to hand at that moment...

I stalked away cursing under my breath, knowing in that moment that if I didn't, the 10ft Amazonian Woman would be the least of her problems!

I'd had enough.

I left soon afterwards with the vow I would never return to hospitality again. Whereas before there had been a calm of enduring customer service, now there was a raging sea, and I just *knew* that if anyone ever treated me like that again they would get more than the tidal wave of my tongue and I wouldn't be able to stop it!

Maybe it was a culmination of factors that brought me to that point. Perhaps my 'Roadhouse' stint had stretched me too far, or it could simply have been that after nearly thirty years in the service industry my time was up.

Whatever the reasoning, my day was done and I went off in a whole new direction with little more than a whole host of memories of the good, the bad, and the downright deplorable.

So as my tale comes to an end, what did I learn from all of this?

Lots.

Firstly, anyone who can remain, or else has no choice than to keep working in the hospitality industry - I salute you. You are the unsung heroes of the hoover, *haute cuisine* and hellish offerings left in beds as hotels the world over reap the rewards of your labours.

And so firstly, let me leave you with this; the Customer may be King, but it is you who are true power behind the throne, and I'm not talking about the ones that come with a dodgy flush and a toilet brush!

Secondly, it came as no small surprise to me years later to discover that skirts aren't actually *too* bad and can be worn comfortably - but only on the proviso they aren't compulsory and go down to the floor! Indeed since my working life began legislation in this country now makes it unlawful to force a woman into a skirt and quite right, too. Shame it came too late in my first bar job, but I had the satisfaction of telling one sexist boss that *no I would not be wearing a skirt* as I ordered a nice pair of trousers.

And last but not least; custard can be lumpy – in fact, there are times when lumpy custard is positively okay, and this, for me, was a welcome revelation in a world where prissiness rules and everything has to be 'just right'.

It was a defining moment, and so Long Live Lumpy Custard and all the 10ft Amazonians who suffer the slings and arrows of 'Custard 'n' Service'!

May your spirit be merry, your mo-jo stay savvy and always *always* - keep a firm hand on your tips!

Printed by Amazon Italia Logistica S.r.l.
Torrazza Piemonte (TO), Italy